# The Emergent Psalter

## Isaac Everett

Church Publishing
NEW YORK

**Psalm texts are based on those of the 1979 Book of Common Prayer as edited by the author.**

Church Publishing, Incorporated.
445 Fifth Avenue
New York, New York 10016

www.churchpublishing.com

Cover design: Robert Scott

Music: All music © 2009 Isaac Everett except:
Psalms 1, 111, 121 © 2009 Lacey Brown; Psalms 6, Public Domain (The Psalters); Psalms 13, 41, 119 © 2009 Isaac Everett and j. Snodgrass

Library of Congress Cataloging-in-Publication Data
Bible. O.T. Psalms. English. Everett. 2009.
The emergent psalter / Isaac Everett.
    p. cm.
Includes bibliographical references (p.    ).
ISBN 978-0-89869-617-2 (pbk.)
1. Psalters. 2. Antiphons (Music)  I. Everett, Isaac. II. Title.
BS1424.E94 2009
264'.15--dc22
                                        2009001194

Printed in the United States of America

5 4 3 2 1

Dedicated to the memory
of Dr. Edwina Wright,
Director of Language Studies at Union Theological Seminary,
whose passion, faith, and brilliance touched all of her students

# Contents

# Acknowledgments

I'd like to thank:

- the Reverend Jennifer Linman and the Church of the Epiphany for their support, both financial and theological. It would never have occurred to me to write this book, or go to seminary, if it had not been for my five years there as an artist-in-residence,
- Troy Messenger and Penna Rose, who read the first draft of this book when it was my master's thesis at Union Theological Seminary and whose input was invaluable,
- Dara Centonze, Stephen Hoevertsz, and Miles Kennedy for taking this music on the road with me,
- Katie Everett for her love, support, and grammar,
- Transmission, for being the community I've always needed and the liturgical laboratory I've always wanted.

# New Traditionalism in the Emerging Church

In recent years, there has been a resurgence of interest in ancient forms of liturgy and spiritual practice, especially within the emergent church,[1] although analogous trends are occurring within Roman Catholicism, Evangelical Protestantism, and even American Judaism and Islam.[2] My generation has been given credit for the renewal of all sorts of liturgical practices, including *lectio divina*, praying the rosary, and consulting spiritual directors.[3] As a recent article in *U.S. News and World Report* stated:

> You see this [trend] quite clearly in the so-called emergent communities, new, largely self-organizing groups of young Christian adults who meet in private homes, church basements, or coffeehouses around the country. So free-form that many don't even have pastors, these groups nevertheless engage in some ancient liturgical practices, including creedal declarations, public confession, and Communion. They may use a piece of a bagel as the body of Christ, but the liturgy is a traditional anchor in services that may include films, skits, or group discussions of a biblical topic.[4]

This return to ancient practice does not necessarily coincide with a return to theological orthodoxy. In fact, emerging Christians are discovering that the mystery and ambiguity of ritual meshes with a postmodern worldview in a way that their past experiences of worship haven't. This renewal of tradition doesn't signify a renewed commitment to religious institutions, either, which are often mistrusted by emerging Christians. Rather than adopt a single liturgical tradition wholesale, emerging Christians are drawing from a variety of traditions to create a personalized, a la carte spiritual practice,[5] and I've seen emergent communities rediscovering everything from incense to altar calls. One common thread, however, is an emphasis on practices that "integrate body and spirit," focusing on actions rather than words, which engage

---

1 Eddie Gibbs and Ryan K. Bolger, *Emerging Churches: Creating Christian Community in Postmodern Cultures* (Grand Rapids, MI: Baker Academic, 2005), 224.
2 Jay Tolson, "A Return to Tradition: A New Interest in Old Ways Takes Root in Catholicism and Many Other Faiths," *U.S. News & World Report* (December 13, 2007), 1.
3 Lauren F. Winner, "Gen X Revisited: A Return to Tradition?" *Christian Century* (117, no. 31, November 8, 2000), 1146.
4 Tolson, "A Return to Tradition," 1.
5 Gibbs and Bolger, *Emerging Churches,* 222.

an entire community in collaborative, interactive worship.[6]

This kind of liturgical innovation is vital to the continuation of any tradition. As Tom Driver writes, "The ability to innovate while at the same time echoing ancient custom is what keeps any tradition alive."[7] Ritual doesn't thrive on endless repetition or on preservation for its own sake, and religious communities that "tenaciously hold to all traditions and refuse to accommodate to the changing environment" are often the quickest to disappear.[8]

The emerging church, of course, is not an organization—it is a loose network held together through word of mouth, blogs, and personal relationships, so there isn't any corporate infrastructure that can facilitate or fund liturgical exploration. Communities frequently lack professional leadership of any kind, whether musical, pastoral, or administrative, and very few emerging Christians have the time and training necessary for creating original music. Additionally, communities that meet in homes tend to lack access to musical instruments, and the only way music is incorporated into worship is by playing canned music in the background. As a result, most of the liturgical output of these communities is in the form of prayers, litanies, and reflections; with a few exceptions, the emerging church has yet to create a musical identity for itself.

It is my sincere hope that this situation will change, for communal singing exemplifies emergent values; it is an ancient practice, it is a physical practice, and it is a communal practice. This project grew out of a desire to address that need, to make an ancient musical practice accessible to small groups of Christians who meet in homes, cafes, and subway tunnels and who don't have the benefit of a choir, an organ, a sound system, or printed bulletins. My own rediscovery of psalm singing came through Transmission,[9] a small emerging house church that meets in upper Manhattan, and Sanctuary, an alternative worship service held by an Episcopal Church on Manhattan's East Side, and most of the music in this book was written for them over the course of the past five years.

The translations of the psalms in this volume are about 80 percent from the Book of Common Prayer and about 20 percent my own. The versification most closely adheres to the Bible. I have also put the psalms into inclusive language as much as possible without destroying the original meaning.

6 Gibbs and Bolger, *Emerging Churches*, 220.
7 Tom F. Driver, *Liberating Rites: Understanding the Transformative Power of Ritual* (Boulder, CO: Westview Press, 1998), 213.
8 Roger Finke, "Innovative Returns to Tradition: Using Core Teachings as the Foundation for Innovative Accommodation." *Journal for the Scientific Study of Religion* (Volume 43, Number 1, March 2004), 5.
9 http://www.transmissioning.org

# A Brief History of
# Psalms and Antiphons

Christians have been singing psalms in worship since the very beginning of Christianity, and the practice began even earlier, at least as early as the Second Temple Period (536 BCE –70 CE). Many of the psalms contain evidence of musical origins, declaring the psalmist's intention to sing and play for God,[10] and making references to psalteries, harps, and other instruments. Although the psalm's superscriptions are a later addition, the fact that many of them refer to the psalms as a שִׁיר or מִזְמוֹר (a song or a hymn) suggests that they were written to be sung.

It is likely, in fact, that the biblical Psalter was not compiled merely for personal devotional use, but rather as a hymnbook for the second temple.[11] Echoes of liturgy can be found within many of the psalms, especially those which record rituals for entry into the temple, such as Psalms 15 and 24.[12] Further, numerous psalms contain repeated refrains that might have been written as congregational antiphons, such as Psalms 42–43 and 135. It is possible, of course, that not every psalm was written for liturgical use in the temple;[13] for example, Psalm 30 seems to have been originally written as the celebratory prayer of an individual, likely in response to a recovery from illness.[14] The superscription of the psalm,[15] however, suggests a liturgical use "at the dedication of the temple," which the Talmud[16] associates with the Temple Dedication Festival, i.e., Chanukah. It is unclear whether this psalm, and others like it, were originally written for individual use and were absorbed by the temple cult or whether they were first written by professional poets on behalf of the Temple. In either case, by the time the biblical Psalter had been compiled, the majority of them had been co-opted for liturgical use.

The Mishnah contains even more accounts of psalms in temple liturgy, reporting that one psalm was assigned for recitation in the temple for each day of the week:

---

10  Sigmund Mowinckel, *The Psalms in Israel's Worship* (Sheffield, England: JSOT Press, 1992), 9.
11  J. Clinton McCann, Jr., "The Book of Psalms: Introduction, Commentary, and Reflections." *The New Interpreter's Bible: Volume 4* (New York: Doubleday, 1992), 642.
12  S. E. Gillingham, *The Poems and Psalms of the Hebrew Bible* (Oxford: Oxford University Press, 1994), 225-226.
13  Massey H. Shepherd, Jr., *The Psalms in Christian Worship: A Practical Guide* (Minneapolis, MN: Augsburg Publishing House, 1976), 19.
14  McCann, *The Book of Psalms,* 795.
15  "A Psalm. A Song at the dedication of the temple. Of David."
16  McCann, *The Book of Psalms,* 795.

These were the Psalms which the Levites used to recite in the Temple; on the first day of the week they used to recite *The Earth Is the Lord's* (24); on the second day, *Great Is The Lord* (48), on the third day *God Standeth In The Congregation of the Mighty* (82); on the fourth day, *God of Vengeance* (94), on the fifth day, *Exult Aloud Unto God Our Strength* (81), on the sixth day, *The Lord Reigneth* (93), and on the Sabbath, *A Psalm, a Song for the Sabbath Day* (92).[17]

Although the Mishnah was compiled in the second century, the Septuagint echos five of these seven assignments (days three and five are absent), suggesting that they actually reflect Second Temple Era liturgy and are not later additions. The Mishnah further agrees that the psalms were sung, not read,[18] and adds that the Levites would blow trumpets after each section.[19]

There is less written in the Mishnah about synagogue worship, but we are told that the Hallel Psalms (113 through 118) were occasionally used in morning services. More importantly, *The Jewish Encyclopedia* states that, rather than being sung by priests,

In the synagogues the Psalms were chanted antiphonally, the congregation often repeating after every verse chanted by the presenter the first verse of the Psalm in question. "Halleluyah" was the word with which the congregation was invited to take part in this chanting. Hence it originally prefaced the Psalms, not, as in the Masoretic text, coming at the end. At the conclusion of the Psalm the presenter added a doxology ending with "and say ye Amen," whereupon the congregation replied "Amen, Amen."[20]

Psalms were also important and recognizable to the early Christians—the New Testament contains no fewer than ninety-three quotes from more than sixty of the psalms.[21] Luke depicts Jesus quoting Psalm 110 from memory,[22] Peter quoting Psalms 16, 132, and 110 from memory,[23] and Paul quoting Psalms 2, 16, and 89, also from memory.[24] Paul observes that when the church at Corinth gathers, "each one has a Psalm, a lesson, a revelation, a tongue, or an interpretation,"[25] implying that the psalms were used in early Christian worship.

The first explicit mention of psalms in Christian liturgy, however, is made by Tertullian, who in his second-century *Treatise on the Soul* describes a charismatic woman in his church and says, "Whether it be in the reading of Scriptures, or in the *chanting of Psalms*, or

17 Tamid 7:4
18 Sukkah 4:5
19 Tamid 7:3
20 Emil G. Hirsch, "Psalms" *Jewish Encyclopedia* (1906, ed. Cyrus Adler, et al.), http://www.jewishencyclopedia.com/view.j sp?artid=574&letter=P&search=Psalms, accessed February 11, 2008.
21 Shepherd, *The Psalms*, 32.
22 Luke 20:41-42
23 Acts 2:14-36
24 Acts 13:33
25 1 Corinthians 14:26 Note that while the NRSV translates the first word as "hymn," the Greek word used by Paul is ψαμον (*psalmos*) which is, of course, the Greek word for Psalm.

in the preaching of sermons, or in the offering up of prayers, in all these religious services matter and opportunity are afforded to her of seeing visions."[26] Tertullian doesn't, however, indicate *how* the psalms were chanted. For this we must turn to the *Apostolic Constitutions,* which describes antiphonal psalm chanting in almost exactly the same way that the Mishnah does: "But when there have been two lessons severally read, let some other person sing the hymns of David, and let the people join at the conclusions of the verses."[27]

The earliest use of psalms in eucharistic liturgies is as a gradual, a text chanted between other scriptural readings.[28] The gradual seems to have been done antiphonally, with a leader chanting the main text of the Psalm and the congregation responding after each verse, or each group of verses, with a fixed refrain.[29] This method of chanting is also attested in the fourth century by Athanasius, who reports, "Now I considered that it would be unreasonable in me to desert the people during such a disturbance, and not to endanger myself in their behalf; therefore I sat down upon my throne, and desired the Deacon to read a Psalm, and the people to answer, 'For His mercy endures for ever,' and then all to withdraw and depart home."[30]

In fact, by the fourth century, after Christianity had become the official religion of the Roman Empire and Western Christian practice began to be standardized, psalm singing was widespread throughout the church.[31] Eusebius comments on this, saying, "The command to sing Psalms in the name of the Lord was obeyed by everyone in every place: for the command to sing is in force in all churches which exist among the nations, not only the Greeks but also the barbarians throughout the whole world, and in towns, villages, and in the fields."[32] In a remarkably detailed account of fourth-century liturgy, *Egeria's Diary of Pilgrimage* notes that "among all these matters takes first place, that proper psalms and antiphons are always sung. Those sung at night or towards the morning, those sung by day at the sixth and ninth hours or at the vespers, continually they are proper and have a meaning pertinent to what is being celebrated."[33] The association of psalms with antiphons was so strong that the fifth-century *Armenian Lectionary of Jerusalem,* which pairs psalms with corresponding readings from the New Testament, identifies the psalms by antiphon rather than by number or by reprinting the entire text.[34]

During the next few centuries, liturgical use of psalms gradually increased, especially in monastic practice. Egyptian monasticism concluded each day with two services, vespers and nocturns, each of which consisted of singing twelve Psalms.[35] By the sixth century, Benedict of Nursia had expanded this to eight daily offices in his rule for

---

26 Tertullian, Treatise on the Soul, Chapter 9, http://www.newadvent.org/fathers/0310.htm, accessed March 11, 2008, emphasis added.
27 Apostolic Constitutions, Book II, section LVII.
28 Shepherd, *The Psalms,* 38.
29 Shepherd, *The Psalms,* 38-39.
30 Athanasius, Apologia de Fuga, 24.
31 Mary Berry, "Psalmody," *A New Dictionary of Liturgy & Worship* (Ed. J. G. Davies, London: SCM Press, 1996), 451.
32 Susan J. White, *Foundations of Christian Worship* (Louisville, KY: Westminster John Knox Press, 2006), 50.
33 Niek A. Schuman, "Paschal Liturgy and Psalmody in Jerusalem 380-384 CE: Some Observations and Implications," *Psalms and Liturgy* (Ed. Dirk J. Human and Cas J. A. Vos, London: T&T Clark International, 2004), 141.
34 Ibid, 144.
35 Shepherd, *The Psalms,* 56-57.

monastic life, and he arranged the 150 psalms within these offices such that the entire biblical Psalter would be sung each week.[36] This tradition slowly influenced the practice of the secular clergy, and by the ninth century all clerics were required to observe the full round of daily offices.[37] Throughout this process, however, it became less and less common for a congregational antiphon to be interspersed throughout the psalm; instead, an antiphon was sung only at the beginning and the end of the text.[38] Throughout the rest of the Middle Ages, the liturgical prominence of the psalms gradually diminished as they were omitted, replaced with canticles, and truncated down to versicles.

Psalms received new life during the Reformation when the appearance of vernacular Psalters allowed the canonical book of Psalms to be reinstated as a congregational hymnal.[39] John Calvin went as far as to declare that psalmody was the only biblically allowed form of liturgical singing.[40] This resurgence was initiated by the publication of *La Forme des Prières et Chants Ecclésiastiques* in 1542, a vernacular Psalter that placed thirty-nine of the psalms into meter, enabling them to be sung to commonly known folk tunes[41] (previously, psalm-singing was limited to arrhythmic chant tones). John Calvin later expanded this into the Genevan Psalter, the final edition of which contains all 150 psalms in rhymed, metrical form. As a liturgical innovation, the Genevan Psalter had far-reaching influence: *Sternhold and Hopkins' Psalter*, published in the late 1540s, was included in most versions of the Anglican Book of Common Prayer, and the *Bay Psalm Book*, another English-language metrical Psalter, was the first book published in America in 1640.

As American Protestantism developed, however, singing traditions such as Wesleyan hymns, shape-note singing, and gospel music quickly eclipsed psalmody as the primary vehicle for liturgical singing. Today, the biblical Psalter is rarely used as a hymnbook, and the tradition of psalm-singing has been relegated nearly exclusively to the world of "high liturgy."

A metrical Psalter, in the tradition of Protestant reformers, would be impractical for us in emerging communities because metrical Psalters set the entire psalm to music, retooling the text into stanzas. Singing the psalm like this requires every participating member of the community to a copy of the text. Instead, the responsorial tradition seems more appropriate—in other words, only one verse is selected and set to music, and the congregation can pick it up by ear. Historical accounts imply that the text of the psalm was typically sung or chanted by a cantor in between congregational refrains, but at Transmission we've found it much easier to only sing the antiphon, reading the text of the psalm over improvised music. We try to avoid paper bulletins at Transmission, since we don't have a photocopier, and following this model all we need is a single copy of *The Emergent Psalter* for the entire community.

36 Shepherd, *The Psalms*, 58.
37 Shepherd, *The Psalms*, 59.
38 John Harper, "Psalmody," *The New Westminster Dictionary of Liturgy and Worship* (ed. Paul Bradshaw, Louisville, KY: Westminster John Knox Press, 2002), 392.
39 Nathan D. Mitchell, "Reforms, Protestant and Catholic," *The Oxford History of Christian Worship* (ed. Geoffrey Wainwright and Karen B. Westerfield Tucker, Oxford: Oxford University Press, 2006), 329.
40 Shepherd, *The Psalms*, 50.
41 Klaus Seybold, *Introducing the Psalms* (London: T&T Clark, 1990), 116-117.

# Goals for
# the Psalter

*The Melodies Must Be Simple.*

These antiphons are intended for congregational singing rather than for performance by a trained cantor, so they need to be doable by people who have no formal training in music. Although any group who wishes to use these melodies will need to have at least one person who can read musical notation, most communities don't have the luxury of a professional musician. Ideally, the melodies will be simple, elegant, and intuitive enough to be learned by ear after a few repetitions.

Following this rule puts me in continuity with the historical traditions of congregational psalmody, which have rarely included melodic virtuosity. According to Mowinckel, the first melodies for the psalms were likely extremely simple, more akin to a recitative than a song,[42] and Augustine reports that Athansius "had the reader of the Psalm utter it with so slight a modulation of the voice that he seemed to be speaking it rather than singing it."[43]

*The Antiphons Must Make Use of Modern Musical Vocabulary.*

I'm not merely trying to resurrect a dead tradition, I'm trying to creatively adapt that tradition for my own community. In 1942, Suzanne Langer famously claimed that music is, in fact, a language.[44] Just as the Alexandrian Jews needed to translate the biblical Psalter into Greek, the Roman Church into Latin, the Reformers into French, and the Anglicans into English, so too must we translate them into our musical context. To do otherwise would be to deny the truth of Pentecost, that the Spirit can and will speak to us in our native tongues, and the truth of incarnation, that traces of God are manifest in our world and in our culture.[45]

More pragmatically, there would be no point in merely imitating past musical styles, since communities who wish to perfectly reconstruct traditional psalmody could simply purchase a copy of the Genevan Psalter or any number of plainsong and Anglican chant Psalters that are still in print. Not only is there no need for another

---

42 Mowinckel, *The Psalms*, 9.
43 Shepherd, *The Psalms*, 39.
44 Lawrence Ferrara, *Philosophy and the Analysis of Music: Bridges to Musical Sound, Form, and Reference* (New York: Excelsior Music Publishing Co., 1991), 13.
45 Tony Jones, *The New Christians: Dispatches from the Emergent Frontier* (San Francisco: Jossey-Bass, 2008), 76.

such Psalter, but an attempt to recreate the style of earlier Psalters would be a denial of my own cultural context and would neglect the playful innovation that Tom Driver suggests is so vital to healthy ritual traditions.[46]

## The Music Must Be Adaptable.

At Transmission, we've sung these psalms a cappella, we've sung them in a park with a guitar, we've sung them gathered around an upright piano, and we've sung them in dance clubs to the thudding bass of a DJ. There is no way of knowing in what contexts these antiphons will be used, so it's important that they be flexible enough to be useable. For the most part, the melodies are diatonic, so they'll work over the written chords, simpler chords, or over a drone pitch. They're also rhythmic enough that they can stand on their own if a community doesn't have access to any sort of musical accompaniment.

## The Antiphons Must Be True to the Biblical Psalter.

The 1907 edition of the *Catholic Encyclopedia* states that:

> The verse which serves as the antiphon text contains the fundamental thought of the Psalm to which it is sung, and indicates the point of view from which it is to be understood. In other words, it gives the key to the liturgical and mystical meaning of the Psalm with regard to the feast on which it occurs.[47]

Discovering the "fundamental thought of the Psalm" is an intimidating goal! Furthermore, I'm enough of a product of postmodernity to think that it's impossible to distill the "fundamental" meaning of any text. The psalms have had many different meanings to many different people over the centuries. For example, the Royal Psalms might have been composed for coronation liturgies, but they were preserved through the exile and in the early church because they were perceived to have a messianic character. So which is the "fundamental" meaning?

Fortunately, my generation is not the first generation to have difficulty discerning the fundamental thought of a psalm. In the ninth century, it was widely believed that all antiphons had their source in a canonical *Liber Antiphonarius*, penned by Gregory the Great himself, even though no one seemed to have ever seen a copy. Amalarius of Metz, an adherent to this view, had questions about antiphons, so he went to Rome in order to procure a copy of this text. Unfortunately, he returned home disappointed and empty-handed, reporting that "his numerous questions to the Roman clergy about the order and arrangement of antiphons were met with mostly inconclusive or vague answers."[48]

Like Amalarius, we have no clear direction when mining psalms for liturgical

---

46 Driver, *Liberating Rites*, 185.
47 Joseph Otten, "Antiphon," *The Catholic Encyclopedia, Volume 1* (New York: Robert Appleton Company, 1907), http://www.newadvent.org/cathen/01575b.htm, accessed March 18, 2008.
48 Timothy Thibodeau, "Western Christendom," *The Oxford History of Christian Worship* (ed. Geoffrey Wainwright and Karen B. Westerfield Tucker, Oxford: Oxford University Press, 2006), 244.

use. Sometimes, a psalm will already contain a repeated refrain that was probably first used as an antiphon. Other times, structural analysis of a psalm will lead to one verse being identified as a lynchpin or a thesis statement. For some psalms, it might make more sense to consider how the psalm is most likely to be used liturgically; perhaps a psalm is always paired with another text in the Revised Common Lectionary, or maybe there is one famous verse in a psalm that is likely to be a favorite. Whatever criterion is eventually used for a particular psalm, however, the text and the composition of the music should strive to account for the original intent of the author.

### *The Psalter Must Honor the Entire Biblical Psalter.*

There is a tendency in churches to ignore the parts of the Bible that we find uncomfortable or embarrassing. At some point in our tradition, we ceased writing songs of "praise and lament" and began writing songs of "praise and worship," a reflection of a wider cultural bias against weakness and vulnerability.[49] In the Christian music industry, there is an understanding that Christian music must be uplifting and positive despite the fact that biblical poetry, especially the psalms, presents anger, grief, and bitterness alongside joy, hope, and praise. This purging of "negativity" implicitly judges how we worship. It says that if we don't feel happy in church then we are not truly worshiping. It says that prayers of anger and prayers of sorrow are not authentic prayers. It says that expressions of joy are activities for the whole community while expressions of sadness are inappropriate for public display. This prejudice is unbiblical.

In his book *The New Christians: Dispatches from the Emergent Frontier*, Tony Jones writes that "emergents embrace the whole Bible, the glory and the pathos."[50] He notes that the Revised Common Lectionary often edits biblical texts, such as on the Feast of Pentecost when all three years of the lectionary proscribe reading "Psalm 104:24–34, 35b," removing references to the destruction of the wicked. Such censorship refuses to acknowledge the flawed humanity made manifest in the psalms and refuses worshipers the experience of wrestling with their own textual tradition. If this Psalter is to be truly useful in Christian practice, it will need to honor grief, anger, and bitterness as valid and healthy expressions of faith.

---

49 I. Nowell, "Psalms, Book of," *New Catholic Encyclopedia: Volume 11, 2ⁿᵈ Ed.* (ed. Berard L. Marthaler, Detroit: Gale Group, 2003), 797.
50 Jones, *The New Christians*, 144.

# Psalm 22:
# A Psalm of Individual Lament

My God, my God, why have you for - sa - ken me?

This psalm, characterized by graphic and evocative depiction of affliction, is most widely known as the psalm that Jesus quotes upon the cross:[51] "My God, my God, why you have forsaken me?" It's usually read on Good Friday, appearing in the Revised Common Lectionary on that day every year. With its imagery of pierced hands and clothing divided by casting lots, this psalm has become so deeply associated with the passion narratives that it is difficult for modern Christians to find anything else in it. Some communities are likely to view parallels between the 22nd Psalm and the Passion narratives as clear indicators of prophecy, while others will follow in the steps of scholars who suggest that the gospel writers inserted references to the psalm into the story in order to help make sense out of Jesus' death.[52]

It's impossible to say what the exact intent of the author was because, as is typical for a lament, the psalm is not clear about what tribulations have befallen the psalmist. The lengthy descriptions of physical suffering could be referring to physical illness, although the repeated references to being mocked by assembled crowds of enemies implies an element of persecution. Some suggest that the psalm had its origin as a folk song written by a peasant farmer who owed large amounts of money and was about to lose his or her land. Other people think that it was written purposefully vague so it could serve as an archetypical lament for liturgical use.[53]

## Exegesis
The 22nd Psalm can be generally classified as a "psalm of individual lament." This classification doesn't rule out the possibility that the psalmist was composing on

---

51 Matthew 27:46, Mark 15:34.
52 John Dominic Crossan, *Who Killed Jesus? Exposing the Roots of Anti-Semitism in the Gospel Story of the Death of Jesus* (San Francisco: HarperSanFrancisco, 1996), 136-137, 141-143, 145.
53 Gillingham, *The Poems and Psalms*, 177-184.

behalf of a community, be it cultic, royal, or otherwise, but instead reflects the fact that the psalmist writes completely in the first person singular. It's a sharp contrast to communal psalms of lament, such as Psalms 44, 80, 94, and 108. Individual laments are by far the most common genre in the Psalter,[54] and they follow a general format of an opening address, a description of affliction, a plea for help, a profession of trust, and a promise to praise or sacrifice to God.[55] There are other literary devices that are typical of laments as well, including exaggerated, metaphorical depictions of the psalmist's suffering, representation of the psalmist's enemies as animals (in this case bulls, dogs, and lions), and attempts to argue God into action.[56]

The 22nd Psalm's "description of affliction" section is notably long, and structurally it can be divided into two distinct arcs. The archetypical cycle of opening address (vv. 1–5), complaint (vv. 6–8), and petition (vv. 9–11) is completed as expected, at which point the psalmist inserts a second section of complaint (vv. 12–18), followed by a second section of petition (vv. 19–21). Only after this double opening does the psalm progress toward the expected profession of trust and the promise of praise and sacrifice. These final elements contain a dramatic shift in tone. The psalm simply shifts directly from the imperative tense (הוֹשִׁיעֵנִי) to the perfect tense (וּמִקַּרְנֵי): "Save me from the mouth of the lion" leads directly into "from the horns of the wild oxen you have rescued me" with no explanation of how, exactly, such a dramatic reversal of circumstance occurred. Just as the exact nature of the psalmist's suffering is left unclear, so too is the mechanism of his or her salvation.

The abrupt shift in tone, along with the double introduction, leads one to wonder if the psalm, in its present form, might be a redaction of two or three unrelated texts. The last third of the psalm shares much in common with other psalms of individual thanksgiving—in fact, the thematic structure is almost identical to Psalms 92 and 138. This section might have been added at a later date; if the original psalm ended with the plea for help, the thanksgiving would have been added to fulfill the expected profession of trust and promise of praise, imposing the archetypical structure of a lament onto the text.

It's not difficult to imagine how this psalm could have lent its narrative structure to the writers of the passion narratives. The initial depiction of affliction correlates with Good Friday as the author recites the experience of physical suffering. The psalm then moves on to the joyous celebration of Easter in verses 22–23, praising God for rescue from death. The final section of the Psalm (25–31) can be interpreted as a foreshadowing of Pentecost—praise is offered on behalf first of the psalmist, then of the congregation of Israel, then of all the nations of the world, and finally of all people in every generation yet to come.

## Antiphonal Text

For the purposes of writing an antiphon, I was caught between a commitment to critical-historical exegesis, which yields little in the way of narrative context, and a commitment to liturgical utility, which almost requires a supercessionist reading. In

54 Gillingham, *The Poems and Psalms,* 231.
55 McCann, "The Book of Psalms," 644-645.
56 Seybold, *Introducing the Psalms,* 116-117.

many communities (including all those that use the Revised Common Lectionary), this text will almost never be separated from the crucifixion, a fact which can't be ignored and must be acknowledged. I do hope, though, that some communities will allow the text to stand on its own, perhaps using its words of lament to give voice to their own experience of suffering. I think it's possible to use the 22nd Psalm and the experience of Jesus on the cross alongside each other without resorting to a supercessionist reading of the texts, and with this goal in mind, it seemed most prudent to use the famous opening line of the psalm for the antiphon. It is the verse that the majority of congregations will expect, and it grants the antiphon the additional flexibility of being usable with the crucifixion narrative, the psalm, or with the two in conjunction.

In the process of setting this verse to music, it was necessary to decide on which syllable to place primary emphasis, which turned out to be very interesting. The question "*Why* have you forsaken me" is very different from "Why have you forsaken *me*?" The first is a theological question—the psalmist is asking how he or she could have ended up in such a rough spot. The second question, on the other hand, places more emphasis on the identity of the psalmist, whether that be David, the anointed King of Israel (to whom the psalm is credited), Jesus the Messiah, or a collective identity of the chosen nation of Israel against its neighbors, and is almost indignant in its tone.

Personally, I found the most intriguing option to be "My God, my God, why have *you* forsaken me?" Being forsaken by the crowds, the mockers, and the bulls is not unbearable for the psalmist, whereas being forsaken by God is the true cause for despair. This interpretation is especially appropriate in the context of the passion narrative, for by the time Jesus utters these words he is not surprised that his disciples and followers have abandoned him; rather, it is God's absence that he laments.

## Antiphonal Music

Although many of the psalms are metrical in Hebrew, with the number of accented syllables per line following a strict pattern, the 22nd Psalm is not one of them.[57] The lack of discernible pattern might be due to the psalm's composite nature, the original meter being lost through the redaction process, or it might reflect the psalm's origin as a folk poem. It is also possible that the lack of meter was an intentional literary device employed by the psalmist. Attempting to reproduce this effect musically is problematic. I could have created an antiphon that was irregular in rhythm, as in art lieder, or I could have given up on rhythm entirely, as in plainsong, but either option would conflict with my goals of (a) keeping the music in a modern vocabulary and (b) making the music easy for untrained congregations to pick up.

So instead of trying to mimic the text's irregularity, I just superimposed an arbitrary rhythm onto the original text. I opted for a fast waltz to convey the unrelenting, turbulent motion that I imagine going through the psalmist's mind as the situation became more and more desperate.

---

57 Gillingham, *The Poems and Psalms*, 67.

# Psalm 23:
# A Psalm of Confidence

The 23rd Psalm poses unique challenges for a composer simply because it is, perhaps, the best known, most used, and most beloved of all the psalms. Holladay calls this psalm an "American Secular Icon,"[58] and it is frequently referenced in popular films (*X-Men 2, Titanic*) and music (Kanye West's "Jesus Walks,"[59] The Eagle's "Long Road Out of Eden"[60]).

Musically, this psalm has been interpreted by many great composers, including Ralph Vaughan Williams, Leonard Bernstein, Duke Ellington, and John Rutter[61]—an intimidating group of predecessors for any musician approaching this psalm. Fortunately, for the purposes of this Psalter it is not necessary to craft a masterpiece; it is important to keep in mind the goals of creating an antiphon that is both useful for worship and true to the biblical text.

As I often do, I started by examining how this psalm was likely to be used in worship. The most common association for this psalm is grief; for English-speaking Christians, the 23rd Psalm is almost exclusively associated with funerals,[62] and it is a traditional part of Yizkor, a Jewish memorial service for lost loved ones (usually parents). The prevalence of the memorial aspect of the 23rd Psalm can be further evidenced by its usage by President George W. Bush on September 11, 2001:

> Tonight, I ask for your prayers for all those who grieve, for the children whose worlds have been shattered, for all whose sense

---

58  William L. Holladay, *The Psalms through Three Thousand Years: Prayerbook of a Cloud of Witnesses* (Minneapolis, MN: Fortress, 1993), 359.
59  *Somebody tell these NIGGAZ! who Kanye West is I walk through the valley of the shadow of death is* (Kanye West, 2004)
60  *Moon shining down through the palms*
    *Shadows moving on the sand*
    *Somebody whispering the 23rd Psalm*
    *Dusty rifle in his trembling hands* (Don Henley, Glenn Frey, Timothy B. Schmit, 2007)
61  *23rd Psalm; Chichester Psalms; Black, Brown, and Beige; Requiem*
62  McCann, "The Book of Psalms," 767.

of safety and security has been threatened. And I pray they will be comforted by a power greater than any of us, spoken through the ages in Psalm 23: "Even though I walk through the valley of the shadow of death, I fear no evil, for You are with me."[63]

It is interesting that a psalm so full of life-related imagery (eating, drinking, resting) can be so completely associated with death and grief.

Liturgically, however, the psalm enjoys much broader use. In the Revised Common Lectionary, it is used to support shepherd imagery in other readings (Easter 4A, 4B, 4C, Proper 11B), banquet imagery (Proper 23A), and stories about David (Lent 4A), and its used a lot in eucharistic liturgies because of its table/banquet imagery. The widespread popularity of this psalm suggests that there is no limit to the number of ways that a worship community might make use of the text, and therefore its antiphon needs to be as flexible as possible.

## Exegesis

Like the 22nd Psalm, the 23rd Psalm has the form of a lament, although the mood of the text is clearly one of confidence rather than lamentation. This expression of confidence follows naturally from the final section of a lament, and it's quite possible that the 23rd Psalm was placed immediately after the 22nd Psalm for exactly this reason.[64] As Gillingham states:

> If the thanksgiving is connected to the lament in that it speaks of an earlier deliverance, the Psalm of confidence is an even more intrinsic part of the lament because it speaks of trust in spite of all appearances—a confidence within the present uncertainties, for those caught in the conflict between faith and experience.[65]

The 23rd Psalm, therefore, can be read as a parody of the formal elements of a lament. Just like a lament, it begins by calling on the name of God. Then, instead of moving into a description of need, it moves into a description of abundance. The expected three-way relationship between the psalmist, God, and the psalmist's enemies is present, but rather than praying for deliverance the psalmist is eating and drinking in the presence of the enemies. The expected animal metaphors are also present, but rather than comparing the enemies to bulls, lions, or dogs, the psalmist himself is compared to a sheep. At the conclusion, the psalm does not explicitly provide the expected vow to offer praise and sacrifice, but it does end with an assertion that the Psalmist will spend many days בְּבֵית-יְהוָה, in the "House of God," a likely reference to the Temple

The connections to the lament tradition become more apparent in Hebrew. In a study on the book of Lamentations, K. Budde identified a metrical pattern of three

63 Bush, George. Address to the Nation, September 11, 2001, http://www.whitehouse.gov/news/releases/2001/09/20010911-16.html, accessed March 11, 2008.
64 McCann, "The Book of Psalms," 769.
65 Gillingham, *The Poems and Psalms*, 224.

stressed syllables followed by two stressed syllables. Such as:

— — —

— —

— — —

— —

Budde identified this pattern as "lamentlike meter," although subsequent scholarship has shown that while it is most often found in laments (the 5th Psalm, Amos 5), its usage is not restricted to them.[66] It is theorized that this meter was especially suited to this genre because of its asymmetry: "the lack of a third matching accent in the second line brought out a sense of unfulfilled hopes."[67] This lamentlike meter is used in all but one line of the 23rd Psalm; verse 4 is written in 2:2 rather than in 3:2.

So we have a psalm written as a lament in form, syntax, and meter—in other words, in every aspect other than content. This unlikely juxtaposition might have been an intentional, stylistic choice on behalf of the Psalmist. An analogy can be made to Marilyn Manson, who sings despairing lyrics over driving dance beats, or John Woo, who uses children's songs as a backdrop for violent action sequences. Ideally, an antiphonal setting for this psalm would echo this contrast, similarly blurring the line between lament and praise.

## Antiphonal Text

When choosing a line from this psalm to develop into an antiphon, I wanted to choose a verse that would not seem out of place at either a funeral or a celebration of the Eucharist, and which could be used by a community or an individual. Many of the lines, such as "the Lord is my shepherd," seem too individual to be useful in corporate worship. "Yea, though I walk through the valley of the shadow of death" is oriented too much toward fear and grief for use in a Eucharist, yet "my cup overflows" leaves little room for its use in funerary liturgies.

The best candidate seems to be the final line, "I will dwell in the house of the Lord forever." While this is a first-person expression of individual piety, it references worship in the temple (a corporate activity) and so makes sense within a modern worship context. Further, in popular understanding the phrase "house of the Lord" is often taken as a reference to heaven, so this phrase would also be appropriate for funerals. Finally, if the redactors of the biblical Psalter did, in fact, intend that the 22nd Psalm and the 23rd Psalm be read as a single narrative unit, then there is pleasant symmetry in the fact that this Psalter uses the first line of the 22nd and the last line of the 23rd.

Unfortunately there is an issue with the translation of this verse—the phrase לְאֹרֶךְ יָמִים, which is usually translated as "forever," would be more accurately translated as "for many days," indicating that this phrase is more likely to refer to a period of worship in the Temple than to an eternity in heaven. It's important to remember

---

66 Gillingham, *The Poems and Psalms,* 53.
67 Ibid., 62.

that, like the Lord's Prayer, many churchgoers have had the King James translation of this psalm memorized since their childhood and find it jarring to adopt any other translation in worship. Retaining the "forever" translation, therefore, has two advantages: it retains an ambiguity that grants the antiphon flexibility of use and it uses the wording most likely to be known by worshipers.

## Antiphonal Music

Since this psalm is classified as a psalm of confidence, it's tempting to write the antiphon in a major key, but this would risk losing the nuance of the lamentlike structure. A minor key, however, would risk betraying the psalm's thematic content. I briefly considered writing the antiphon in an "in-between" mode, such as mixolydian or dorian, but none of the melodies I wrote seemed to contain the ambiguity I was looking for. I chose instead to have the antiphon subtly move back and forth between the major and minor tonalities. Moving between parallel modes was too blatant a device (and might be too difficult for an average congregation), so instead I put the ambiguity in the underlying chords.[68]

The antiphon is written in Ab major, yet the first chord is the relative minor, F minor. The melody itself resolves to a C, a note common to both keys but which is a root in neither, creating further ambiguity between the two tonalities. It is possible to hear the music in either key, as follows:

| | |
|---|---|
| Ab: | vi—iii—IV—I—V |
| Fm: | i—v—VI—III—VII[69] |

The chords never resolve into a definitive cadence; when the chord cycle is looped, the effect is a perpetual V—vi, i.e., a deceptive cadence.

I also wanted to preserve the asymmetric quality of the original Hebrew meter. The 3:2 meter is not preserved in the English translation, but even if it were, its limping quality would likely be lost if the text were set to a four-bar phrase, and so I chose instead to represent the Hebrew meter with musical phrasing. Although the antiphon is notated as a bar of 4/4, followed by a bar of 2/4, followed by another bar of 4/4, a more intuitive way to understand the phrase is as five half-note pulses with the melody set over the first three and the latter two allowing it to breathe. The fact is that the last two pulses are in the only bar to contain the tonic and the dominant further adds to the ambiguous tonality. This unrelenting lack of resolution is meant to echo the unresolved quality and "unfulfilled hopes"[70] of the 3:2 meter.

---

68  Parallel modes are scales that share the same tonic (root) but have different pitches, such as Ab major and Ab minor.
    Relative modes are scales which share the same notes but have different tonics (roots), such as Ab major and F minor.
69  In Roman numeral notation, capital letters are used to signify major chords while lower-case letters are used for minor chords.
70  Gillingham, *The Poems and Psalms*, 62.

# Psalm 119:
# A Torah Psalm

All who know your voice and lis - ten ar - dent - ly up - hold your laws, bind - ing
El - e - vate my un - der - stand - ing. Ev - er in my heart keep watch. Find my
I was lost, a - lone and hurt - ing; in my heart, you spoke to me. Jus - ti -
Mind - ful of your truth in - side me, med - i - tate with ev - ery breath need - ing
Quake with right - eous in - dig - na - tion, qui - et my frus - tra - tion now, ral - lied
While in time of tri - al, I give ex - al - ta - tion, thanks, and praise, yearn - ing

to the heart your wis - dom, base their lives up - on your cause. Cau - tion
strength in your com - mand - ments for your truth is all I've sought. Give me
fy your hum - ble ser - vant, ju - bi - lant in your de - crees. Kin - dle
on - ly you to guide me nev - er turn - ing from your path. Oth - ers
by your pro - cla - ma - tions, ren - der - ing my sol - emn vows. Save your
al - ways for your guid - ance, zea - lous to the end of days.

those who scorn your teach - ings. Coun - cil me to share your words. Dwel - ling
strength in days of test - ing. Guide me through the deep dis - tress. Hear my
me with strength and pa - tience. Keep me from the an - gry throng! Like the
try, with lies en - snare me. On - ly you can get me through. Pass - ing
ser - vant ev - er faith - ful. Take me from this place of pain. Un - der

in the dust, I hear you deep with - in, and I'm as - sured.
call a - wake and rest - ing, help me strug - gle through this mess.
moun - tains as you raised them, lift me up and hold me strong.
through my plight and pe - ril, per - se - vere for love of you.
your de - fense I'm a - ble. Vin - di - cate me in your name.

By far the longest psalm in the Psalter (and the longest chapter in the Bible), Psalm 119 is unusual in many ways. Although it was clearly written as a single poetic unit, the Revised Common Lectionary hardly ever uses more than eight verses at a time, which prevents congregations from really experiencing the repetitious, complex structure of the psalm on a holistic level. The Orthodox Church, on the other hand, reads the entire psalm on Holy Saturday, and I would advocate reading the entire psalm once a year rather than breaking it up into little bits and sprinkling them throughout the lectionary.

The text itself is broken into twenty-two stanzas of eight verses apiece—one stanza for each of the letters of the Hebrew alphabet. Every verse begins with the letter associated with the stanza—if it were written in English, the first eight verses would start with A, followed by eight verses that start with B, and so on through the entire alphabet. Further, almost every line contains one of eight synonyms for Torah: decrees, precepts, statutes, commandments, ordinances, law, word, and promise. The overall effect is rather dizzying in its relentless reinforcement of the importance of obeying God and seeking out a deeper understanding of God's commandments.

## Exegesis

Since this psalm is based on the Hebrew alphabet, and since it is so concerned with instructing its audience in the ways of God, some scholars suspect that it was written as an educational tool, teaching young students their letters while imparting religious values. When read in that light, it does have a certain "eat your vegetables" vibe to it, and there is one tradition that says King David wrote this psalm while teaching Solomon to read.

Other scholars, however, suggest that memorizing all 176 verses of this psalm would be far more difficult than simply memorizing the alphabet, and doubt that it was written for didactic purposes.[71] Instead, it might have been written as a display of artistic ability, or simply for the amusement of the author. In either case, it is worth noting that although the psalmist uses the word Torah (literally, "teaching"), he or she isn't necessarily referring to the five Books of Moses; the psalmist has a much more expansive understanding of where the Word of God can be found.

## Antiphonal Text

The uniformity of the psalm's message would have made it easy to invent an antiphon that would summarize the entire psalm. When Charles Villiers Stanford set this psalm to music, he never made it past the first verse and when Thomas Attwood did it, he only used verse 33! Still, I felt that selecting a single verse for the antiphon wouldn't do justice to the complexity of the original text and so I decided to make a different antiphon for each stanza. This led to the idea of making the antiphons themselves acrostic. Of course, it wouldn't make sense to have an acrostic collection of antiphons unless they made sense when read

71 Seybold, *Introducing the Psalms*, 44-47.

in succession. And for that to make sense musically, though, the antiphons would have to be metrical and rhyme with one another.

It quickly became apparent this was getting out hand, so I called my friend j. Snodgrass, a remarkably talented wordsmith who has written the lyrics to most of my music since we met a few years ago. After I described what I wanted, he told me that it was ". . . impossible." Three days later, he e-mailed me the text in its final form:

**1–16**

All who know your voice and listen
Ardently uphold your laws
Binding to the heart your wisdom
Base our lives upon your cause

**17–32**

Caution those who scorn your teachings
Counsel me to share your words
Dwelling in the dust, I hear you
Deep within and I'm assured

**33–48**

Elevate my understanding
Ever in my heart keep watch
Find my strength in your commandments
For your truth is all I've sought

**49–64**

Give me strength in days of testing
Guide me through the deep distress
Hear my call awake and resting
Help me struggle through this mess

**65–80**

I was lost, alone and hurting
In my heart you spoke to me
Justify your humble servant
Jubilant in your decrees

**81–96**

Kindle me with strength and patience
Keep me from the angry throng
Like the mountains as you raised them
Lift me up and hold me strong

**97–112**

Mindful of your truth inside me
Meditate with every breath
Needing only you to guide me
Never turning from your path

**113–128**

Others try, with lies ensnare me
Only you can get me through
Passing through my plight and peril
Persevere for love of you

**129–144**

Quake with righteous indignation
Quiet my frustration now
Rallied by your proclamations
Rendering my solemn vows

**145–160**

Save your servant ever faithful
Take me from this place of pain
Under your defense I'm able
Vindicate me in your name

**161–176**

While in time of trial I give
Exaltation, thanks and praise
Yearning always for your guidance
Zealous to the end of days

## Antiphonal Music

It was important to me that each antiphon be able to stand alone and be useable in normal liturgy, but I also wanted to be able to string them together to form a singable hymn. Since the original Hebrew is so repetitive and meant to get stuck in your head, I wrote a simple, folksy tune that can be hummed while walking down the street or sung in Sunday school with minimal accompaniment. The antiphons themselves alternate between two melodies; if the song is sung as a hymn, they act like an A and B section, and if they are used as antiphons while the entire psalm is read, the alternations introduce some much needed variation for what is likely to be a very long reading.

It is worth pointing out that j. Snodgrass's adaptation is writing in 8.7.8.7 meter, which means that any number of well-known hymn tunes could be substituted. I particularly recommend *Hyfrydol* ("Alleluia, Sing to Jesus") or *Nettleton* ("Come Thou Fount of Every Blessing"), each of which shares the A/B structure, or "Will the Circle Be Unbroken," which doesn't.

# Psalm 148:
# A Psalm of Praise

Praise the name of the Lord, whose splen-dor is o-ver earth and hea-ven!

In contrast to Psalms 22 and 23, the 148th Psalm comes with much less liturgical and cultural baggage. It's not a psalm that many people know by heart, nor is it quoted directly in the New Testament. The 148th Psalm is placed in the middle of a five-psalm cluster of praise hymns, all of which begin with "Hallelujah." This cluster concludes the canonical book of Psalms, and at first glance it could be seen as a little more than a happy epilogue, placed at the end of the book to counterbalance the weight of all the laments that precede it. Just as the majority of laments end with a thanksgiving, and just as a psalm of confidence can be read as the answer to a psalm of lament, so does this five-psalm cluster serve as the conclusion to the biblical Psalter; it is a final response to the "theological crises" portrayed in the psalms that lead up to it.[72]

This triumphalist song of praise is heard once a year in churches that follow the Revised Common Lectionary, on the first Sunday after Christmas, a day when stories are told of angels and shepherds, trumpets and anthems. There is a great deal more to this text, however, than simple celebration.

## Exegesis

This psalm follows exactly the archetypical structure for a psalm of praise, beginning with an invitation to praise God, continuing by stating reasons why God is worthy of that praise, and concluding with another invitation to praise God.[73] Psalm 148 is unusual, however, in the length of the initial invitation to praise,[74] which extends through verse 12—nearly the entire psalm. Invitations to praise are directed at nearly everything imaginable, beginning with angels, sun, moon, and stars, continuing

---

72 McCann, "The Book of Psalms," 1271.
73 Gillingham, *The Poems and Psalms*, 208.
74 McCann, "The Book of Psalms," 1271.

with the waters above the heavens, oceans, and sea monsters, continuing further with mountains, trees, birds, and animals, and finally concluding with the kings, princes, commoners, and youths.

It is important to notice that these invitations follow the following pattern: (1) things of the sky, (2) things of the sea, (3) things of the land, and (4) humanity. This is the exact same pattern as is found in the first creation account in Genesis, although the creation story doubles the pattern:

| Sky | light<br>day<br>night | Genesis 1:1–5 | Heavens<br>angels<br>sun<br>moon<br>stars<br>skies | Psalm 148:1–4 |
|------|------|------|------|------|
| Sea | the firmament, separating water from water | Genesis 1:6–8 | sea creatures<br>ocean depths<br>clouds<br>stormy winds | Psalm 148:7–8 |
| Land | dry land<br>growing plants<br>fruit trees | Genesis 1:9–13 | mountains<br>hills<br>fruit trees<br>cedars<br>wild animals<br>cattle<br>small creatures<br>flying birds | Psalm 148:9–10 |
| Sky | stars<br>sun/moon<br>day/night | Genesis 1:14–19 | | |
| Sea | sea beasts<br>birds | Genesis 1:20–23 | | |
| Land | cattle<br>creeping things<br>wild animals | Genesis 1:24–25 | | |
| Humanity | human beings<br>male and female | Genesis 1:26–27 | kings of the earth<br>princes<br>rulers<br>young men<br>maidens<br>old men<br>children | Psalm 148:11–12 |

After verse 12, the parallel continues as the psalmist writes that God's glory is "above the earth and heavens" (עַל-אֶרֶץ וְשָׁמָיִם) using the exact same words as the first verse of Genesis (אֵת הַשָּׁמַיִם וְאֵת הָאָרֶץ). By evoking the creation narrative, the psalmist reminds the listener that God is more powerful than anything on this earth, including the kings, princes, and rulers of humanity. It is more than a song of jubilant victory; it is a bolstering message of hope to discouraged, afflicted, and oppressed people.

This interpretation of the psalm is evidenced by the Song of the Three Jews, a prayer found in the Septuagint's translation of the book of Daniel. The three Jews in question are Shadrach, Meshach, and Abednego, and in the story they have been thrown into a furnace by King Nebuchadnezzar for their refusal to worship a golden statue. The Mazoretic text does not narrate what happens in the furnace, allowing us to only glimpse from the outside that a mysterious fourth figure is seen walking through the fire and that the three Jews later emerge unharmed.[75] The Septuagint, however, allows us to overhear the prayers that Shadrach, Meshach, and Abednego utter within the flames. A majority of the song is taken, line for line, from the 148th Psalm as the three Jews extol the heavens, the angels, the sun, the moon, the sea creatures, the mountains, the hills, et al., to bless the Lord.[76] By using this psalm as an expression of confidence in the face of crushing adversity, the three Jews are reminded that their God is mightier than their tormenter and mightier than the flames of the furnace.

## Antiphonal Text

Unlike the Mazoretic version, in the Song of the Three Jews each line is answered with the refrain "sing praise to him and highly exalt him forever," which is repeated no less than thirty-one times. Within the Septuagint is preserved an example of a liturgical psalm as it would be performed with a responsorial antiphon. The temptation to use a variation of "sing praise to him and highly exalt him forever" as an antiphonal text was quite strong since this seemed to be the antiphon in use by the Greek-speaking Jews who composed the Septuagint, and if the refrain were more interesting I would have used it. Unfortunately, it is a rather unremarkable refrain that would fit with any number of the canonical psalms, and since the vast majority of congregations who will use this Psalter will never encounter the Septuagint, the connection between the texts would not be made. It seemed more prudent to stay within the canonical text of the psalm.

Selecting a single verse from the invitational section of the psalm would limit the scope of the imagery; a verse that only referenced sky, sea, or land would not encompass the message that *all* creation is (or should be) praising the Lord. On the other hand, ignoring the cosmic quality of the first section by choosing a verse from the middle section of the psalm would lose the underlying sense of perspective that gave encouragement against adversity to the Three.

I ended up using a modification of verse 13: "Praise the name of the Lord, whose splendor is over earth and heaven." This verse is the pivot point at which the psalm switches from the first section (invitation to praise) to the second section (reasons why God is worthy of praise), and the antiphon contains one clause of each. It retains the reference to Genesis 1:1 and reminds us that God is more powerful than any problem we might face on this earth.

---

75 Daniel 3:19-30
76 Prayer of Azariah 35-65

## Antiphonal Music

Unlike the 23rd Psalm, the 148th Psalm is written with strong parallelism; with the exception of the last two, every verse has two clauses, nearly synonymous in meaning, with the second being a stronger restatement of the first. The Hebrew meter is 3:3—both halves of each parallel verse contain three accented syllables. Together, these syntactical choices give the text a feeling of symmetry and completeness; nowhere does one encounter the "sense of unfulfilled hope" present in the 23rd Psalm. 3:3 meter is, in fact, quite common for hymns of praise and it is attested in many other psalms, hymns, and even Hebrew prose, including most of the other psalms in this cluster (147, 149, and 150).[77] After much lament, the book of Psalms ends on a strong, confident, reassuring tone; if there were ever an appropriate time for major keys, strong cadences, and 4/4 time, this is it.

And yet I didn't want to pen a melody that ignored the difficult realities faced by those who have made use of this psalm for strength. Rather than use a pure major scale, therefore, I used a traditional middle-eastern mode called *hejas*; a predominantly major tonality that is darkened by a flattened sixth.[78]

---

77 Gillingham, *The Poems and Psalms,* 59.
78 for example, C – D – E – F – G – Ab – B/Bb – C. The seventh tone can be natural or flat depending on context.

# Book I

**1**

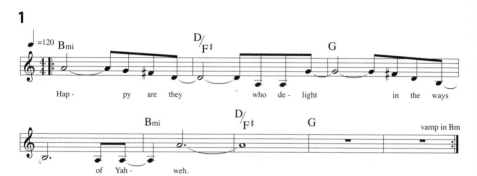

Hap - py are they who de - light in the ways

of Yah - weh.

1  Happy are they
        who have not walked in the counsel of the wicked,
        nor lingered in the way of sinners,
        nor sat in the seats of the scornful!
2        Their delight is in the law of God,
        and they meditate on God's law day and night.
3  They are like trees
        planted by streams of water,
        bearing fruit in due season,
        with leaves that do not wither;
        everything they do shall prosper.

**antiphon**

4  It is not so with the wicked;
        they are like chaff which the wind blows away.
5  Therefore the wicked shall not stand upright when judgment comes,
        nor the sinner in the council of the righteous.
6  For God knows the way of the righteous,
        but the way of the wicked is doomed.

**antiphon**

The Psalter opens by telling us that those who study the teaching of God (literally "the Torah of God") will be happy and blessed. It's not an accident that this psalm was placed first—it's meant to be an introduction to the rest of the book, and it tells us why studying the psalms is a good idea in the first place.

This antiphon was written by Lacey Brown, a fabulous musician from Church of the Apostles in Seattle. Although almost all of the antiphons in this book are mine, I thought that starting with a collaboration would get things started off on a positive note.

## 2

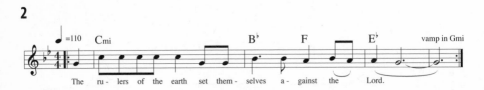

The ru - lers of the earth set them - selves a - gainst the Lord.

1   Why are the nations in an uproar?
    Why do the peoples mutter empty threats?
2   Why do the kings of the earth rise up in revolt,
    and the princes plot together,
    against God and God's Anointed?
3   "Let us break their yoke," they say;
    "Let us cast off their bonds from us."
4   The One whose throne is in heaven is laughing;
    God has them in derision.
5   Then speaks to them in wrath,
    rage fills them with terror.
6   "I myself have set my king
    upon my holy hill of Zion."

**antiphon**

7   Let me announce the decree of God:
    who said to me,
    "You are my Son;
    this day have I begotten you.
8   Ask of me,
    and I will give you the nations for your inheritance
    and the ends of the earth for your possession.
9   You shall crush them with an iron rod
    and shatter them like a piece of pottery."

**antiphon**

10  And now, you kings, be wise;
        be warned, you rulers of the earth.
11      Submit to God with fear,
        and with trembling bow before him;
12      lest God be angry and you perish;
        for God's wrath is quickly kindled.
        Happy are they all who take refuge in God!

**antiphon**

    *So if Psalm 1 serves as an introduction to the whole Psalter, Psalm 2 continues the introduction by summarizing the content of the Psalter; namely, that God is sovereign, higher and mightier than the rulers of the earth. The psalm ends with "Happy are they who take refuge in God," which is probably a reference to the opening of Psalm 1, and an indication that whoever first compiled the Psalter expected these two psalms to be read together.*

## 3   A Psalm of David when he fled from his son Absalom.

1   God, how many adversaries I have!
    How many there are who rise up against me!
2       How many there are who say of me,
        "There is no help for him in his God."
3   But you, O God, are a shield about me;
        you are my glory, the one who lifts up my head.
4   I call aloud upon God,
        who answers me from the holy hill;
5   I lie down and go to sleep;
        I wake again, because God sustains me.
6   I do not fear the multitudes of people
        who set themselves against me all around.

**antiphon**

7   Rise up, O God;
    Set me free, O my God;

Surely, you will strike all my enemies across the face,
>
> you will break the teeth of the wicked.

8     Deliverance belongs to God.
>
> Your blessing be upon your people!

**antiphon**

*In 2 Samuel 15, Absalom, the son of King David, launches a propaganda campaign to convince the Israelites that David isn't listening to their petitions. Absalom follows up with a casual, "If I were judge in the land, all who had a suit could come to me and I would give them justice." It isn't long before the hearts of Israel are set on revolution, and David is forced to flee Jerusalem.*

*Since it is his enemy's slanderous words that have hurt him so badly, it isn't surprising that David is asking God to strike his enemy's cheeks and teeth. The imagery is so brutal—it's not a fate I'd wish on anyone. For better or worse, this psalm was omitted from the lectionary so this antiphon is not likely to be sung often on Sundays.*

## 4     To the leader: with stringed instruments. A Psalm of David.

1     Answer me when I call,
>
> O God, defender of my cause;

You set me free when I am hard-pressed;
>
> have mercy on me and hear my prayer.

2     "You mortals, how long will you dishonor my glory;
>
> how long will you worship dumb idols
>
> and run after false gods?"

3     Know that God does wonders for the faithful;
>
> when I call upon God, I am heard.

4     Tremble, then, and do not sin;
>
> speak to your heart in silence upon your bed.

5     Offer the appointed sacrifices
>
> and put your trust in God.

**antiphon**

6     Many are saying, "Oh, that we might see better times!"
>
> Lift up the light of your countenance upon us, O God.

7    You have put gladness in my heart,
          more than when grain and wine and oil increase.
8    I lie down in peace; at once I fall asleep;
          for only you, God, make me dwell in safety.

**antiphon**

*The beginning of this psalm makes a fine antiphon, but it also works well as a response to prayers. I sometimes use it as a sung response during the prayers of the people, a litany, and other petitional liturgies.*

# 5    To the leader: for the flutes. A Psalm of David.

1    Give ear to my words, O God;
          consider my meditation.
2    Hearken to my cry for help,
          my Ruler and my God,
          for I make my prayer to you.
3    In the morning, God, you hear my voice;
          early in the morning I make my appeal and watch for you.

**antiphon**

4    For you are not a God who takes pleasure in wickedness,
          and evil cannot dwell with you.
5        Braggarts cannot stand in your sight.
     You hate all those who work wickedness.
6        You destroy those who speak lies;
          the bloodthirsty and deceitful, O God, you abhor.

**antiphon**

7    But as for me, through the greatness of your mercy I will go into your house;
        I will bow down toward your holy temple in awe of you.
8    Lead me, O God, in your righteousness,
        because of those who lie in wait for me,
        make your way straight before me.
9    For there is no truth in their mouths;
        there is destruction in their hearts.
        Their throats are open graves;
        they flatter with their tongues.
10   Declare them guilty, O God;
        let them fall, because of their schemes.
        Because of their many transgressions cast them out,
        for they have rebelled against you.
11   But all who take refuge in you will be glad;
        they will sing out their joy forever.
        You will shelter them,
        so that those who love your Name may exult in you.
12   For you, O God, will bless the righteous;
        you will defend them with your favor as with a shield.

**antiphon**

*The last three psalms have all made it pretty clear that following God isn't always easy and sometimes comes with a price. In this case, that price is persecution and slander. Apparently this psalmist didn't get the memo about praying for our enemies.*

**6**    **To the leader: with stringed instruments:**
**according to The Sheminith. A Psalm of David.**

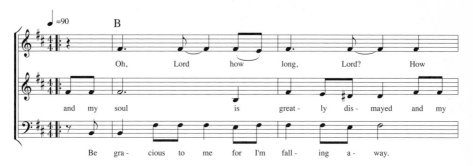

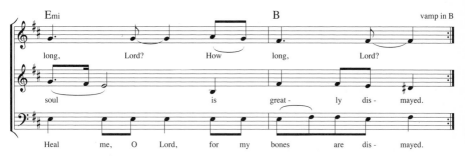

1    God, do not rebuke me in your anger;
do not punish me in your wrath.

2    Have pity on me, God, for I am weak;
heal me, God, for my bones are racked.

3    My spirit shakes with terror;
how long, O God, how long?

4    Turn, O God, and deliver me;
Save me for your mercy's sake.

5    For in death no one remembers you;
and who will give you thanks in the grave?

**antiphon**

6    I grow weary because of my groaning;
every night I drench my bed
and flood my couch with tears.

7    My eyes are wasted with grief
and worn away because of all my enemies.

8    Depart from me, all evildoers,
for God has heard the sound of my weeping.

9    God has heard my supplication;
        God accepts my prayer.
10   All my enemies shall be confounded and quake with fear;
        they shall turn back and suddenly be put to shame.

**antiphon**

*This is the first of the seven "Penitential Psalms," a Christian categorization that goes back at least as far as Cassiodorus in the seventh century. This three-part antiphon comes from the* Divine Liturgy of the Wretched Exiles, *an incredible album by the Psalters, a nomadic group of musicians dedicated to living out the gospel in radical ways. I had the pleasure of opening for the Psalters at a festival last summer and was blown away by this piece of music. Unfortunately, it's hard to capture its flavor in musical notation, but it's about the closest thing to wailing and gnashing of teeth that I've ever heard.*

*I highly encourage you to check out their music at* http://www.psalters.com. *They put all of their music in the public domain and don't charge for their albums, so make sure you give a donation while you're there.*

# 7    A Shiggaion of David, which he sang to God concerning Cush, a Benjaminite.

My God, in you I take re - fuge. Save and de - liv - er me.

1    O God, my God, I take refuge in you;
        save and deliver me from all who pursue me;
2        lest like a lion they tear me in pieces
        and snatch me away with none to deliver me.
3    O God, my God, if I have done these things,
        if there is any wickedness in my hands,
4        if I have repaid my friend with evil
        or plundered him who without cause is my enemy,
5        then let my enemy pursue and overtake me,
        trample my life into the ground,
        and lay my honor in the dust.

**antiphon**

6    Stand up, O God, in your wrath;
        rise up against the fury of my enemies.
        Awake, O my God, decree justice;
7        let the assembly of the peoples gather round you.
        Be seated on your lofty throne, O Most High;
8    O God, judge the nations.
        Give judgment for me according to my righteousness, O God,
        and according to my innocence, O Most High.
9    Let the malice of the wicked come to an end.
    But establish the righteous.
    For you test the mind and heart,
        O righteous God.
10   God is my shield and defense;
        God is the savior of the true in heart.
11   God is a righteous judge;
        God sits in judgment every day.
12   If they will not repent, God will whet a sword;
        and bend a bow, making it ready.
13   God has prepared weapons of death;
        and makes arrows as shafts of fire.

**antiphon**

14   Look at those who are in labor with wickedness,
        who conceive evil, and give birth to lies.
15   They dig a pit and make it deep
        and fall into the hole that they have made.
16   Their malice turns back upon their own heads;
        their violence falls on their own scalps.
17   I will bear witness that God is righteous;
        I will praise the Name of God Most High.

**antiphon**

*No one knows the story of David and Cush, the Benjaminite. There is no consensus on what a Shiggaion is, either.*

## 8    To the leader: according to The Gittith. A Psalm of David.

1    O God our sovereign,
        how great is your Name in all the Earth!
2    Out of the mouths of infants and children
        your majesty is praised above the heavens.
    You have set up a stronghold against your adversaries,
        to quell the enemy and the avenger.

**antiphon**

3    When I consider your heavens, the work of your fingers,
        the moon and the stars you have set in their courses,
4        What is humanity that you should be mindful of them?
        the children of humanity that you should seek them out?
5        You have made humanity little lower than the angels;
        you adorn them with glory and honor.
6        You give them mastery over the works of your hands;
        you put all things under their feet:
7        all sheep and oxen,
        even the wild beasts of the field,
8        the birds of the air, the fish of the sea,
        and whatsoever walks in the paths of the sea.
9    O God our sovereign,
        how great is your Name in all the Earth!

**antiphon**

This is the first example in the Psalter of an antiphon being recorded directly into the text. Notice that the first verse is the same as the last verse; this is a device that occurs quite a bit in the Psalter. The antiphon itself doesn't have much to do with the psalm, which celebrates the incredible honors God has given humanity while remembering that humanity is small compared to the universe.

In 1969, when Buzz Aldrin and Neal Armstrong first landed on the moon, they left a disk with goodwill messages from seventy-three different nations. The Vatican (technically a nation) sent this psalm as their contribution.

## 9    To the leader: according to Muth-labben. A Psalm of David.

1    I will give thanks to you, O God, with my whole heart;
        I will tell of all your marvelous works.
2    I will be glad and rejoice in you;
        I will sing to your Name, O Most High.

**antiphon**

3    When my enemies are driven back,
        they will stumble and perish at your presence.
4    For you have maintained my right and my cause;
        you sit upon your throne judging right.
5    You have rebuked the ungodly
        and destroyed the wicked;
        you have blotted out their names forever and ever.
6    As for the enemy, they are finished,
        in perpetual ruin,
        their cities plowed under,
        the memory of them perished.

**antiphon**

7    But God is enthroned forever;
        God has set up this throne for judgment.
8    It is God who rules the world with righteousness,
        who judges the peoples with equity.
9    God will be a refuge for the oppressed,
        a refuge in time of trouble.
10    Those who know your Name will put their trust in you,
        for you never forsake those who seek you, O God.
11    Sing praise to God who dwells in Zion;
        proclaim to the peoples the things God has done.

12  The Avenger of blood will remember them;
        and will not forget the cry of the afflicted.

**antiphon**

13  Have pity on me, O God;
        see the misery I suffer from those who hate me,
        you who lift me up from the gate of death,
14      so that I may tell of all your praises
        and rejoice in your salvation
        in the gates of the city of Zion.
15  The ungodly have fallen into the pit they dug,
        and in the snare they set their own foot is caught.
16  God is known
        by acts of justice;
        the wicked are trapped in the works of their own hands.
17  The wicked shall be given over to the grave,
        and also all the people that forget God.
18  For the needy shall not always be forgotten,
        and the hope of the poor shall not perish forever.
19  Rise up, O God,
        let not the ungodly have the upper hand;
        let them be judged before you.
20  Put fear upon them, O God;
        let the ungodly know they are but mortal.

**antiphon**

*Psalms 9 and 10 are actually a single psalm, and in the Septuagint (the Greek translation of the Hebrew Bible used by the early Christians), the two are combined. It's clear that they form a single unit because the combined text is an acrostic, with the first letter of each verse forming the Hebrew alphabet: Psalm 9 is roughly A–K and Psalm 10 is roughly L–Z. It was probably split because the two halves have different themes; Psalm 9 is more of a thanksgiving while Psalm 10 is more of a lament. Most modern hymn writers would probably make a theological statement by putting the lament before the thanksgiving, but that's not always the way life works.*

**10**

Why do you stand far a - way? Why do you hide in trou - bl - ing times?

1   Why do you stand so far off, O God,
      and hide yourself in time of trouble?
2   The wicked arrogantly persecute the poor,
      but they are trapped in schemes of their own devising.
3   The wicked boast of their heart's desire;
      the covetous curse and revile God.
4   The wicked are so proud
      that they care not for God;
      their only thought is,
      "God does not matter."

**antiphon**

5   Their ways are devious at all times;
      your judgments are far above, out of their sight;
      they defy all their enemies.
6   They say in their heart, "I shall not be shaken;
      no harm shall happen to me ever."
7   Their mouth is full of cursing, deceit, and oppression;
      under their tongues are mischief and wrong.
8   They lurk in ambush in public squares
      and in secret places they murder the innocent;
      they spy out the helpless.
9   They lie in wait, like a lion in a covert;
      they lie in wait to seize upon the lowly;
      they seize the lowly and drag them away in their net.
10    The innocent are broken and humbled before them;
      the helpless fall before their power.
11  They say in their hearts, "God has forgotten;
      and has hidden God's face; God will never notice."

**antiphon**

12  Rise up, O God!
    Lift up your hand, O God!
    Do not forget the afflicted!
13  Why should the wicked revile God?
        Why should they say in their heart, "You do not care"?
14  Surely, you behold trouble and misery.
    You see it and take it into your own hand.
    The helpless commit themselves to you,
        for you are the helper of orphans.
15  Break the power of the wicked and evil;
        search out their wickedness
        until you find none.

**antiphon**

16  God is sovereign forever and ever;
        the ungodly shall perish from the land.
17  God will hear the desire of the humble;
        you will strengthen their heart
        and your ears shall hear
18      to give justice to the orphan and oppressed,
        so that mere mortals may strike terror no more.

**antiphon**

*To reflect that these two psalms are actually a single psalm, albeit with different emphases, I used the same melody for each antiphon, putting the thanksgiving in major and the lament in minor. Some people might object to accusing God of hiding during times of trouble but, hey, it's from the Bible! Sadly, those people will probably never see it since Psalm 10 was suspiciously omitted from the Revised Common Lectionary.*

*In worship, I encourage you to use both psalms back to back, switching modes and antiphons at the halfway mark.*

## 11    To the leader. Of David.

1   In God I take refuge;
> how then can you say to me,
> "Fly away like a bird to the hilltop;
2   For see how the wicked bend the bow
> and fit their arrows to the string,
> to shoot from ambush at the true of heart.
3   When the foundations are being destroyed,
> what can the righteous do?"

**antiphon**


4   God is in the holy temple;
> God's throne is in heaven.
> God's eyes behold the inhabited world;
> God's piercing eye weighs our worth.
5   God weighs the righteous as well as the wicked,
> but those who delight in violence are abhorred.
6   Upon the wicked God shall rain coals of fire and burning sulphur;
> a scorching wind shall be their lot.
7   For God is righteous;
> and delights in righteous deeds;
> and the just shall see God's face.

**antiphon**


*In the face of wickedness, violence, poverty, despair, militarism, and oppression, this psalm encourages us not to give up the fight, nor to hide where we are comfortable and safe.*

## 12   To the leader: according to The Sheminith. A Psalm of David.

1   Help me, God,
    for there is no godly one left;
        the faithful have vanished from among us.
2   Everyone speaks falsely with neighbors;
        with a smooth tongue
        they speak from a double heart.
3   Oh, that God would cut off all smooth tongues,
        and close the lips that utter proud boasts!
4   Those who say, "With our tongue will we prevail;
        our lips are our own; who is God over us?"

**antiphon**

5   "Because the needy are oppressed, and the poor cry out in misery,
        I will arise," says God,
        "and give them the help they long for."
6   The words of God are pure words,
        like silver refined from ore
        and purified seven times in the fire.
7   O God, watch over us
        and save us from this generation forever.
8   The wicked prowl on every side,
        and that which is worthless is highly prized by everyone.

**antiphon**

*This is an excellent example of how the psalms can be God speaking to us as well as us speaking to God. It begins by imploring God for help and then confidently asserts a promise of deliverance on God's behalf. It seems that by presuming to speak for God, the psalmist might be overstepping a bit, but it's also important to remember that we are often called to be the hand of God in the world. If, as the body of Christ, we make the effort to take care of the poor and the needy, then this promise is being fulfilled.*

## 13    To the leader. A Psalm of David.

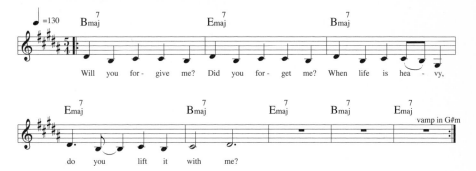

♩=130

Bmaj7        Emaj7        Bmaj7

Will you for - give me? Did you for - get me? When life is hea - vy,

Emaj7    Bmaj7    Emaj7    Bmaj7    Emaj7

vamp in G#m

do you lift it with me?

1    How long, O God? will you forget me forever?
     How long will you hide your face from me?
2    How long shall I have perplexity in my mind,
          and grief in my heart, day after day?
     How long shall my enemy triumph over me?
3    Look upon me and answer me, O God, my God.
     Give light to my eyes,
          lest I sleep in death;
4          Lest my enemy say, "I have prevailed,"
     and my foes rejoice that I have fallen.

**antiphon**

5    But I put my trust in your mercy;
          my heart is joyful because of your saving help.
6    I will sing to God, for dealing with me richly;
          I will praise the Name of God Most High.

**antiphon**

*In seminary, one of my professors, Dr. David Carr, had us rewrite psalms in the spirit of Ernesto Cardenal, who in his book* Salmos *creatively rewrote many psalms to reflect the struggle for liberation in his native Nicaragua. I chose to use this psalm, and my retooling of it eventually became a song, "Thirteen," on my second album,* Transmission. *This is the chorus of that song.*

*Don't be intimidated by the odd time signature—it looks more difficult than it is.*

## 14    To the leader. Of David.

Ps. 14: Fools say in their hearts, "There is no God!"

Ps. 53: When God's peo - ple are re - stored,

Ev - ery - one's cor - rupt, no one does good."

Ja - cob will re - joice.

1    The fool has said in his heart,
        "There is no God."
    All are corrupt and commit abominable acts;
        there is none who does any good.

2    God looks down from heaven upon us all,
        to see if there are any who are wise,
        if there is one who seeks after God.

3    Every one has proved faithless;
        all alike have turned bad;
        there is none who does good;
        no, not one.

4    Have they no knowledge, all those evildoers
        who eat up my people like bread
        and do not call upon God?

5    See how they tremble with fear,
        because God is in the company of the righteous.

6    Their aim is to confound the plans of the afflicted,
        but God is their refuge.

**antiphon**

7    Oh, that Israel's deliverance would come out of Zion!
        when God restores the fortunes of his people,
        Jacob will rejoice and Israel be glad.

**antiphon**

Biblical Hebrew doesn't have much in the way of punctuation. Because of this, there's no way to tell when the quote in verse 1 ends. The opening lines of this psalm could be translated:

> Fools say in their hearts, "There is no God." All are corrupt, they
> do abominable deeds; there is no one who does good.

But moving the punctuation around, the verses could also be translated:

> Fools say in their hearts, "There is no God. All are corrupt, they
> do abominable deeds; there is no one who does good."

Further, the NRSV chooses "they" instead of "all," which implies that it is the fools who are corrupt.

Personally, I think that this second might be the intention of the author. In either case, there is clearly a strong connection between "there is no God" and "there is no one who does good." In Hebrew they are אֵין אֱלֹהִים (ein elohim) and אֵין עֹשֵׂה-טוֹב (ein ose-tov) respectively; notice how they have the exact same structure, vowel sounds, and number of syllables. Under this interpretation, it seems as if the corruption and complete lack of goodness experienced by the "fools" is leading them to deny the existence of God.

In New York, I have certainly heard people say, "How can you believe in a good and just God in a world with so much wickedness and suffering?" and "How can you subscribe to a religion that has been so hypocritical, abusive, and corrupt?" It's hardly surprising that nonbelievers judge a religion by looking at the people who practice and espouse it.

I'm not entirely comfortable calling those people fools, however. What's foolish about judging a tree by the fruit it bears? Perhaps the foolishness lies in judging an entire tree by a few of its fruit. The foolishness isn't "corruption and sin exist" but rather "everyone is corrupt." That's when we move from disillusionment to cynicism, one of the most paralyzing feelings a young person can feel.

For an alternate antiphon, check out Psalm 53, which is almost the exact same psalm. It has a slightly different take on the text, but uses the same meter and chords. Adventurous congregations can sing them together for some haunting counterpoint, as printed with Psalm 53.

## 15   A Psalm of David.

Who may a - bide? on your ho - ly hill?

1   God, who may dwell in your tabernacle?
    who may abide upon your holy hill?
2   Whoever leads a blameless life
    and does what is right,
    who speaks the truth from the heart,
3   with no guile upon the tongue,
    who does no evil to friends,
    who does not heap contempt upon neighbors,
4   in whose sight the wicked are rejected,
    but who honors those who fear God,
    who has sworn to do no wrong
    and does not take back a word,
5   who does not give money in hope of gain,
    nor take a bribe against the innocent.
    Whoever does these things shall never be overthrown.

**antiphon**

*This is an Entrance Liturgy, probably sung by pilgrims seeking admittance to the Temple on Zion. The call and response in this psalm makes me wonder if the first verse was originally an antiphon, or at least a prompt by the gatekeeper for a response from the pilgrim. The psalm lists a variety of things that qualify one to ascend the hill, but I left the antiphon open-ended by only including the question.*

## 16   A Miktam of David.

My heart is glad, my soul re - joi - ces, my bo - dy rests se - cure.

1   Protect me, O God, for I take refuge in you;
2   I have said to God,
    "You are my God, my benefactor;
    none are above you."

3    All my delight is upon the godly that are in the land,
           upon those who are noble among the people.
4           But those who run after other gods
              shall have their troubles multiplied.
       Their libations of blood I will not offer,
              nor take the names of their gods upon my lips.
5    O God, you are my portion and my cup;
           it is you who uphold my lot.
6    My boundaries enclose a pleasant land;
           indeed, I have a goodly heritage.

**antiphon**

7    I will bless God who gives me counsel;
           my heart teaches me, night after night.
8    I have set God always before me;
           because God is at my right hand, I shall not fall.
9    My heart, therefore, is glad,
           and my spirit rejoices;
           my body also rests in hope.
10   For you will not abandon me to the grave,
           nor let your holy one see the Pit.
11   You will show me the path of life.
       In your presence there is fullness of joy,
           and in your right hand are pleasures for evermore.

**antiphon**

*This confident affirmation of faith is used by some emergent communities as an alternative to the Nicene Creed.*

## 17　A Prayer of David.

1　Hear my plea of innocence, O God;
　　give heed to my cry; listen to my prayer,
　　which does not come from lying lips.

2　Let my vindication come forth from your presence;
　　let your eyes be fixed on justice.

3　Weigh my heart, summon me by night,
　　melt me down; you will find no impurity in me.

4　I give no offense with my mouth as others do;
　　I have heeded the words of your lips.

5　My footsteps hold fast to the ways of your law;
　　in your paths my feet shall not stumble.


**antiphon**


6　I call upon you, O God,
　　for you will answer me;
　　incline your ear to me
　　and hear my words.

7　Show me your marvelous loving-kindness,
　　O savior of those who take refuge at your right hand
　　from those who rise up against them.

8　Keep me as the apple of your eye;
　　hide me under the shadow of your wings,

9　　from the wicked who assault me,
　　from my deadly enemies who surround me.

10　They have closed their hearts to pity,
　　and their mouths speak proud things.

11　　They press me hard, now they surround me,
　　watching how they may cast me to the ground,

12    Like a lion, greedy for its prey,
            and like a young lion lurking in secret places.

**antiphon**

13    Arise, O God; confront them.
        Bring them down;
            deliver me from the wicked by your sword.
14    Deliver me, O God, by your hand
            from those whose portion in life is this world;
            Whose bellies you fill with your treasure,
            who are well supplied with children
            and leave their wealth to their little ones.
15    But at my vindication I shall see your face;
            when I awake, I shall be satisfied, beholding your likeness.

**antiphon**

*J. Clinton McCann Jr. (see bibliography) points out that this psalm has a chiasm, a symmetrical literary device that introduces elements while building toward a climax, and then reprises those elements in reverse order after the climax. It's a device that is used frequently in the Hebrew Bible, especially in Genesis.*

*A the psalmist's nonviolence (v. 4)*
*B the psalmist's stability (v. 5)*
*C the psalmist's humble speech (v. 6)*
*D the central petition (vv. 7–9)*
*C' the wicked's arrogant speech (v. 10)*
*B' the wicked's attempt to destabilize (v. 11)*
*A' the wicked's violence (v. 12)*

*This makes "D," the plea to be held under God's wing like young birds with their mother, the climax of the psalm.*

**18**  **For the leader. Of David, the servant of God, who addressed the words of this song to God after God had saved him from the hands of all his enemies and from the clutches of Saul. He said:**

God, you are my strength, my rock, my for-tress and de-liv-er-er.

God, you are my rock, my shield, the horn of my sal-va-tion.

1   I love you, O God my strength,
      O God my stronghold, my crag, and my haven.
2      My God, my rock in whom I put my trust,
      my shield, the horn of my salvation, and my refuge.
   You are worthy of praise.
3   I will call upon God,
      and so shall I be saved from my enemies.
4   The breakers of death rolled over me,
      and the torrents of oblivion made me afraid.
5      The cords of hell entangled me,
      and the snares of death were set for me.
6   I called upon God in my distress
      and cried out to my God for help.
      God heard my voice from the heavenly dwelling;
      my cry of anguish came to God's ears.

**antiphon**

7      The earth reeled and rocked;
      the roots of the mountains shook;
      they reeled because of his anger.
8      Smoke rose from God's nostrils
      and a consuming fire out of God's mouth;
      hot burning coals blazed forth.
9   God parted the heavens and came down
      with a storm cloud underfoot.

10   God mounted on cherubim and flew;
          swooping on the wings of the wind.
11   God was wrapped in darkness,
          and made dark waters and thick clouds a pavilion.

**antiphon**

12   From the brightness of God's presence, through the clouds,
          burst hailstones and coals of fire.
13   God thundered out of heaven;
          the Most High uttered a voice.
14   God loosed arrows and scattered them;
          and hurled thunderbolts and routed them.
15   The beds of the seas were uncovered,
          and the foundations of the world laid bare,
          at your battle cry, O God,
          at the blast of the breath of your nostrils.
16   God reached down from on high and grasped me;
          and drew me out of great waters.
17      God delivered me from my strong enemies
          and from those who hated me
          for they were too mighty for me.
18   They confronted me in the day of my disaster;
          but God was my support.
19   God brought me out into an open place;
          and rescued me because he delighted in me.

**antiphon**

20   God rewarded me because of my righteous dealing;
          because my hands were clean I was rewarded;
21      For I have kept the ways of God
          and have not offended against my God;
22      For all God's judgments are before my eyes,
          and I have not put God's decrees away from me;
23   For I have been blameless
          and have kept myself from iniquity;
24   Therefore God rewarded me according to my righteous dealing,
          because of the cleanness of my hands.
25   With the faithful you show yourself faithful, O God;
          with the forthright you show yourself forthright.

26 With the pure you show yourself pure,
  but with the crooked you are wily.
27 You will save a lowly people,
  but you will humble the haughty eyes.

**antiphon**

28 You, O God, are my lamp;
  my God, you make my darkness bright.
29 With you I will break down an enclosure;
  with the help of my God I will scale any wall.
30 God's ways are perfect;
  the words of God are tried in the fire;
  God is a shield to all who trust.
31 For who is God, but God?
  who is the Rock, except our God?
32 It is God who girds me about with strength
  and makes my way secure.
33 God makes me sure-footed like a deer
  and lets me stand firm on the heights.
34 God trains my hands for battle
  and my arms for bending even a bow of bronze.

**antiphon**

35 You have given me your shield of victory;
  your right hand also sustains me;
  your loving care makes me great.
36 You lengthen my stride beneath me,
  and my ankles do not give way.
37 I pursue my enemies and overtake them;
  I will not turn back till I have destroyed them.
38 I strike them down,
  and they cannot rise;
  they fall defeated at my feet.
39 You have girded me with strength for the battle;
  you have cast down my adversaries beneath me;
40 you have put my enemies to flight.
  I destroy those who hate me.

**antiphon**

41   They cry out, but there is none to help them;
       they cry to God, who does not answer.
42   I beat them small like dust before the wind;
       I trample them like mud in the streets.
43   You deliver me from the strife of the peoples;
       you put me at the head of the nations.
       A people I have not known shall serve me.
44   No sooner shall they hear than they shall obey me;
       strangers will cringe before me.
45      The foreign peoples will lose heart;
       they shall come trembling out of their strongholds.

**antiphon**

46   God lives! Blessed is my Rock!
     Exalted is the God of my salvation!
47      God gave me victory
       and cast down the peoples beneath me.
48      You rescued me from the fury of my enemies;
       you exalted me above those who rose against me;
       you saved me from my deadly foe.
49   Therefore will I extol you among the nations, O God,
       and sing praises to your Name.
50   God multiplies the victories of the king;
       and shows loving-kindness to the anointed,
       to David and his descendants forever.

**antiphon**

    *The first two verses contain the longest set of epithets in the Bible. People of faith are always inventing new metaphors for God, which is a good thing. I am bit puzzled by those who are vehemently opposed to feminine images for God, though—if we can refer to God as a rock, a horn, or a shield with a straight face (or, for that matter, as a lamb, a shepherd, a vine, or a gate), why can't we refer to God as a mother?*
    *This psalm is spoken by David in 2 Samuel 22.*

## 19  To the leader. A Psalm of David.

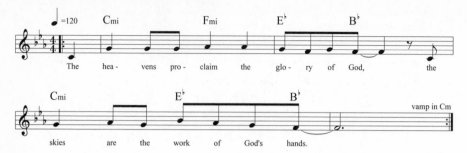

1   The heavens declare the glory of God,
        and skies are the work of God's hands.
2   One day tells its tale to another,
        and one night imparts knowledge to another.
3   Although they have no words or language,
        and their voices are not heard,
4   Their sound has gone out into all lands,
        and their message to the ends of the world.
    In the deep God has set a pavilion for the sun;
5       it comes forth like a bridegroom out of his chamber;
        it rejoices like a champion to run its course.
6   It goes forth from the uttermost edge of the heavens
        and runs about to the end of it again;
        nothing is hidden from its burning heat.


**antiphon**


7   The law of God is perfect
        and renews life;
        the testimony of God is sure
        and gives wisdom to the innocent.
8   The statutes of God are just
        and rejoice the heart;
        the commandment of God is clear
        and gives light to the eyes.
9   The fear of God is clean
        and endures forever;
        the judgments of God are true
        and righteous altogether.

10        More to be desired are they than gold,
          more than much fine gold,
          sweeter far than honey,
          than honey in the comb.

**antiphon**

11   By them also is your servant enlightened,
          and in keeping them there is great reward.
12   Who can tell how often he offends?
      Cleanse me from my secret faults.
13     Above all, keep your servant from presumptuous sins;
          let them not get dominion over me;
          then shall I be whole and sound,
          and innocent of a great offense.
14   Let the words of my mouth
          and the meditation of my heart
          be acceptable in your sight,
          O God, my strength and my redeemer.

**antiphon**

*Verse 14 is often used by preachers immediately before delivering a sermon. If you want to make that prayer the focus of the psalm rather than the magnificence of the heavens, I suggest using the chorus from The Melodians' "Rivers of Babylon" as an antiphon. People in my generation will probably know the cover by Sublime better than the original.*

## 20    To the leader. A Psalm of David.

1   May God answer you in the day of trouble,
        the Name of the God of Jacob defend you;
2   Send you help from the holy place
        and strengthen you out of Zion;
3   Remember all your offerings
        and accept your burnt sacrifice;
4   Grant you your heart's desire
        and prosper all your plans.
5   We will shout for joy at your victory
        and triumph in the Name of our God;
        may God grant all your requests.

**antiphon**

6   Now I know that God gives victory to the anointed;
        and will answer out of holy heaven,
        with the victorious strength of God's right hand.
7   Some put their trust in chariots and some in horses,
        but we will call upon the Name of God our God.
8   They collapse and fall down,
        but we will arise and stand upright.
9   O God, give victory to the king.
    Answer us when we call.

**antiphon**

*Horses, chariots, tanks, and bombs will all collapse, so we shouldn't build our world on these things. A militaristic society is a house built on sand, and this psalm reminds us of that.*

## 21  To the leader. A Psalm of David.

We will sing and chant the prais - es of your might - y deeds.

1   The king rejoices in your strength, O God;
      how greatly he exults in your victory!
2   You have given him his heart's desire;
      you have not denied him the request of his lips.
3   For you meet him with blessings of prosperity,
      and set a crown of fine gold upon his head.
4   He asked you for life, and you gave it to him:
      length of days, forever and ever.
5   His honor is great, because of your victory;
      splendor and majesty have you bestowed upon him.
6   For you will give him everlasting felicity
      and will make him glad with the joy of your presence.
7   For the king puts his trust in God;
      because of the loving-kindness of the Most High,
      he will not fall.

**antiphon**

8   Your hand will lay hold upon all your enemies;
      your right hand will seize all those who hate you.
9   You will make them like a fiery furnace
      at the time of your appearing, O God;
    You will swallow them up in your wrath,
      and fire shall consume them.
10   You will destroy their offspring from the land
      and their descendants from among the peoples of the earth.
11   Though they intend evil against you
      and devise wicked schemes,
      yet they shall not prevail.
12   For you will put them to flight
      and aim your arrows at them.

**antiphon**

13   Be exalted, O God, in your might;

        we will sing and praise your power.

**antiphon**

*This is a psalm that I really wouldn't mind removing from the Psalter—it's a Royal Psalm, all about the divine right of the earthly ruler and how God will destroy that ruler's enemies, but doesn't have much about love for those enemies or the ethical obligations of that ruler. Then I noticed that the word "praise" in the last verse is not* hallel, *the word I was expecting, but rather* נְזַמְּרָה, *from the root* zamar, *which can also mean "to trim or prune."*

*As soon as I realized this, the alternate translation of "we will trim and prune your mighty deeds" leapt into my head—just what I'd be doing if I skipped over this psalm. It's dishonest if we pretend this stuff isn't in the Bible.*

## 22    To the leader: according to The Deer of the Dawn. A Psalm of David.

1    My God, my God,

        why have you forsaken me?

        Why are so far from my cry

        and from the words of my distress?

2    O my God,

        I cry in the daytime, but you do not answer;

        by night as well, but I find no rest.

3    Yet you are the Holy One,

        enthroned

        upon the praises of Israel.

4    Our ancestors put their trust in you;

        they trusted, and you delivered them.

5    They cried out to you

        and were delivered;

        they trusted in you

        and were not put to shame.

**antiphon**

6    But as for me, I am a worm, not a human,
        scorned by all and despised by the people.

7    All who see me laugh me to scorn;
        they curl their lips
        and wag their heads, saying,

8    "You trusted in God;
        let God deliver you;
        let God rescue you,
        if God delights in you."

9    Yet you are the one who took me out of the womb,
        and kept me safe upon my mother's breast.

10  I have been entrusted to you ever since I was born;
        you were my God when I was still in my mother's womb.

11  Be not far from me,
        for trouble is near,
        and there is none to help.

12  Many young bulls encircle me;
        strong bulls of Bashan surround me.

13  They open wide their jaws at me,
        like ravening and roaring lions.

**antiphon**

14  I am poured out like water;
        all my bones are out of joint;
        my heart within my breast
        is melting wax.

15      My mouth is dried out like a pot-sherd;
        my tongue sticks to the roof of my mouth;
        and you have laid me in the dust of the grave.

16  Packs of dogs close me in,
        and gangs of evildoers circle around me;
        they pierce my hands and my feet;

17  I can count all my bones.
        They stare and gloat over me.

18  They divide my garments among them;
        they cast lots for my clothing.

**antiphon**

19  Be not far away, O God;
        you are my strength; hasten to help me.

20 Save me from the sword,
       my life from the power of the dog.
21 Save me from the lion's mouth,
       my wretched body from the horns of wild bulls.
22 I will declare your Name to my brethren;
       in the midst of the congregation I will praise you.

**antiphon**

23 Praise God, you that fear;
       stand in awe, O offspring of Israel;
       all you of Jacob's line, give glory.
24 For God does not despise nor abhor the poor in their poverty;
       neither hide from them;
       but when they cry God hears them.
25 My praise is of God in the great assembly;
       I will perform my vows in the presence of those who worship.
26 The poor shall eat and be satisfied,
       and those who seek God shall praise:
"May your heart live forever!"

**antiphon**

27 All the ends of the earth shall remember and turn to God,
       and all the families of the nations bow down.
28      For sovereignty belongs to God
       who rules over the nations.
29 All who sleep in the earth bow down in worship to God alone;
       all who go down to the dust
       fall before God.
30 My descendants shall serve God;
       they shall be known as God's forever.
31      They shall come and make known to a people yet unborn
       the saving deeds that God has done.

**antiphon**

*This psalm was covered pretty thoroughly in the introduction, but I should add that this antiphon was used as the chorus for "Execution," a track from my first album,* Rotation. *For the verses, the song uses a metrical version of Psalm 22 by Isaac Watts, penned in 1719.*

## 23    A Psalm of David.

1    God is my shepherd;
        I shall not be in want.
2    God makes me lie down in green pastures
        and leads me beside still waters.
3        God renews my life
        and guides me along right pathways
        for the sake of God's Name.
4    Though I walk through the valley of the shadow of death,
        I shall fear no evil; for you are with me;
        your rod and your staff, they comfort me.

**antiphon**

5    You spread a table before me in the presence of those who trouble me;
        you have anointed my head with oil,
        and my cup overflows.
6    Surely your goodness and mercy shall follow me
        all the days of my life,
        and I will dwell in the house of God
        forever.

**antiphon**

*This is one psalm that you should make the effort to hear in Hebrew; it's wonderfully elegant. For the example, the first two lines, which we usually hear as "The Lord is my shepherd, I shall not be in want," is only four words in Hebrew. If only that simplicity could be communicated in English!*

## 24    Of David. A Psalm.

1 The earth is God's and all that is in it,
    the world and all who dwell therein.
2 For it is God who founded it upon the seas
    and made it firm upon the rivers of the deep.

**antiphon**

3 "Who can ascend the hill of God?
  Who can stand in the holy place?"
4 "Those who have clean hands and a pure heart,
    who have not pledged themselves to falsehood,
    nor sworn by what is a fraud.
5 They shall receive a blessing from God
    and a just reward from the God of their salvation."
6 Such is the generation of those who seek him,
    of those who seek your face, O God of Jacob.

**antiphon**

7 Lift up your heads, O gates!
  Lift them high, O everlasting doors;
    and the ruler of glory shall come in.
8 "Who is this ruler of glory?"
    "God, strong and mighty,
    God, mighty in battle."
9 Lift up your heads, O gates;
  lift them high, O everlasting doors;
    and the ruler of glory shall come in.
10 "Who is this ruler of glory?"
    "The God of hosts
    is the ruler of glory."

**antiphon**

*This is the other Entrance Liturgy (along with Psalm 15). Obviously, we don't know exactly how it was used, but the text has a lot of questions followed by answers, making me wonder if it was originally a call-and-response, like the Sursum Corda ("The Lord be with you, and also with you," etc.) or any number of gospel songs. You can sing this antiphon either way.*

## 25   Of David.

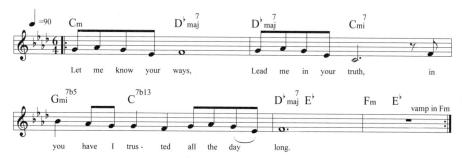

1    To you, O God, I set my hope in you;
2        my God, I put my trust in you;
        let me not be humiliated,
            nor let my enemies triumph over me.
3    Let none who look to you be put to shame;
        let the treacherous be disappointed in their schemes.
4    Show me your ways, O God,
        and teach me your paths.
5        Lead me in your truth and teach me,
        for you are the God of my salvation;
            in you have I trusted all the day long.

**antiphon**

6    Remember, O God,
        your compassion and love,
            for they are from everlasting.
7    Remember not the sins of my youth and my transgressions;
        remember me according to your love
            and for the sake of your goodness, O God.
8    Gracious and upright is God;
        who teaches sinners the way;
9    Who guides the humble in doing right
        and teaches the way to the lowly.

10   All the paths of God are love and faithfulness
        to those who keep the covenant and testimonies.

**antiphon**

11   For your Name's sake, O God,
        forgive my sin, for it is great.
12   Who are they who fear God?
        God will teach them the way that they should choose.
13   They shall dwell in prosperity,
        and their offspring shall inherit the land.
14   God is a friend to those who fear
        and will show them the covenant.

**antiphon**

15   My eyes are ever looking to God,
        who shall pluck my feet out of the net.
16   Turn to me and have pity on me,
        for I am left alone and in misery.
17   The sorrows of my heart have increased;
        bring me out of my troubles.
18   Look upon my adversity and misery
        and forgive me all my sin.
19   Look upon my enemies, for they are many,
        and they bear a violent hatred against me.
20   Protect my life and deliver me;
        let me not be put to shame,
        for I have trusted in you.
21   Let integrity and uprightness preserve me,
        for my hope has been in you.
22        Deliver Israel, O God,
        out of all its troubles.

**antiphon**

*We saw earlier that Psalm 9–10 is an acrostic poem, and here we have our second. If you aren't familiar with acrostics, they are poems in which the first letter of each line forms a hidden message, like the Dutch National Anthem. In the Psalter, acrostic poems spell out the twenty-two-letter Hebrew alphabet from start to finish and might have been used as memory aids to children learning to read.*

## 26    Of David.

I've set my eyes on your love. I walk in faith-ful-ness to you.

1    Give judgment to me, O God,
      for I have lived with integrity;
      I have trusted in you
      and have not faltered.

2    Test me, O God, and try me;
      examine my heart and my mind.

3          For your love is before my eyes;
      I have walked faithfully with you.

4    I have not sat with scoundrels,
      nor do I consort with the deceitful.

5          I have hated the company of evildoers;
      I will not sit down with the wicked.

6          I will wash my hands in innocence, O God,
      that I may go in procession round your altar,

7          singing aloud a song of thanksgiving
      and recounting all your wonderful deeds.

**antiphon**

8    God, I love the house in which you dwell
      and the place where your glory abides.

9    Do not sweep me away with sinners,
      nor my life with those who thirst for blood,

10         Whose hands are full of evil plots,
      and their right hand full of bribes.

11   As for me, I will live with integrity;
      redeem me, O God, and have pity on me.

12   My foot stands on level ground.
      I will bless God in the full assembly.

**antiphon**

*Many people think that this psalm, like Psalm 7, is a prayer of someone who has
been falsely accused, but I think it depicts someone going to the temple to worship. The text
contains fragments of ritual such as walking to the temple, washing one's hands, walking*

*around the altar, singing songs, and blessing among the great congregation. This would be an excellent psalm for a processional, a call to worship, or for walking a labyrinth.*

*For Sunday worship, this text is often paired with Matthew 16, in which Jesus sets his sights on Jerusalem, much to the dismay of his disciples, and I can imagine him praying this psalm as he begins walking toward his death. I tried to write an antiphon that would be appropriate for either use.*

## 27   Of David.

The Lord is the strength of my life, of whom shall I be a - fraid?

1   God is my light and my salvation;
       whom shall I fear?
    God is the strength of my life;
       of whom shall I be afraid?
2   When evildoers came upon me
       to eat up my flesh,
       it was they, my foes and my adversaries,
       who stumbled and fell.
3   Though an army should encamp against me,
       yet my heart shall not be afraid;
       And though war should rise up against me,
       yet will I put my trust in God.

**antiphon**

4   One thing have I asked of God;
       one thing I seek;
       that I may dwell in the house of God
       all the days of my life,
       to behold the fair beauty of God
       and to seek God in the temple.
5   For God shall keep me safe in shelter;
       in the day of trouble
       hide me in the secrecy of a dwelling
       and set me high upon a rock.

6    Even now God lifts my head up
         above my enemies round about me.
         Therefore I will sacrifice in God's tent with shouts of joy
         I will sing and make music to God.

**antiphon**

7    Hearken to my voice, O God, when I call;
         have mercy on me and answer me.
8    You speak in my heart and say,
         "Seek my face."
     Your face, God, will I seek.
9    Hide not your face from me,
         nor turn away your servant in displeasure.
         You have been my helper.
     Cast me not away; do not forsake me,
         O God of my salvation.
10   Though my father and my mother forsake me,
         God will sustain me.
11   Show me your way, O God;
         lead me on a level path,
         because of my enemies.
12   Deliver me not into the hand of my adversaries,
         for false witnesses have risen up against me,
         and also those who speak malice.

**antiphon**

13   What if I had not believed
         that I should see the goodness of God
         in the land of the living!
14   O tarry and await God's pleasure;
         be strong, and God shall comfort your heart;
     Wait patiently.

**antiphon**

*This potent psalm expresses a radical hope for deliverance. The author is apparently the victim of false accusations, a difficulty that seems to plague many of the psalmists.*

## 28    Of David.

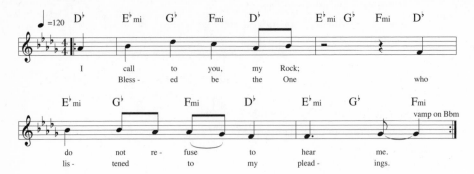

1    O God, I call to you;
> my Rock, do not be deaf to my cry;
> lest, if you do not hear me,
> I become like those who go down to the Pit.

2    Hear the voice of my prayer
> when I cry out to you,
> when I lift up my hands
> to your holy of holies.

3    Do not snatch me away with the wicked or with the evildoers,
> who speak peaceably with their neighbors,
> while strife is in their hearts.

4    Repay them according to their deeds,
> and according to the wickedness of their actions.
> According to the work of their hands repay them,
> and give them their just deserts.

5    They have no understanding of God's doings,
> nor of the works of God's hands;
> therefore God will break them down
> and not build them up.

**antiphon**

6    Blessed is God!
> who has heard the voice of my prayer.

7    God is my strength and my shield;
> in whom my heart trusts,
> I have been helped; therefore my heart dances for joy,
> and in my song I will praise.

8    God is the strength of the people,
> a safe refuge for the anointed.

9    Save your people and bless your inheritance;
         shepherd them and carry them forever.

**antiphon**

*This psalm breaks neatly into two pieces. Verse 1 implores God to not refuse to hear the prayers of the psalmist while verse 6 announces that God has, in fact, heard the sound of the psalmist's pleadings. The antiphon can switch texts after verse 5 to reflect this, or the two texts can be done each time, one after the other.*

## 29    A Psalm of David.

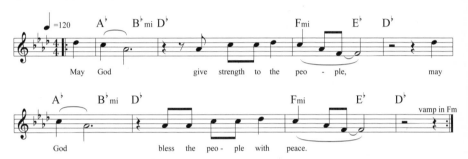

1    Ascribe to God, you gods,
         ascribe to God glory and strength.
2    Ascribe to God the glory due the Name;
         worship God in the beauty of holiness.

**antiphon**

3    The voice of God is upon the waters;
         the God of glory thunders;
         God is upon the mighty waters.
4    The voice of God is a powerful voice;
         the voice of God is a voice of splendor.
5        The voice of God breaks the cedar trees;
         God breaks the cedars of Lebanon;
6    God makes Lebanon skip like a calf,
         and Sirion like a young wild ox.
7    The voice of God splits the flames of fire;
8        the voice of God shakes the wilderness;
         God shakes the wilderness of Kadesh.

9     The voice of God makes the oak trees writhe
        and strips the forests bare.
        And in the temple of God all are crying, "Glory!"
10   God sits enthroned above the flood;
        God sits enthroned as ruler for evermore.

**antiphon**

11   God shall give strength to the people;
        God shall give the people the blessing of peace.

**antiphon**

*Many scholars think that this is the oldest psalm in the Psalter due to its archaic language, heavy repetition, and its description of YHWH as a storm god, similar to Baal or Hadad. The final couplet, wishing peace on the people, comes as a bit of a surprise to me after so much imagery of power and destruction.*

## 30   A Psalm. A Song at the dedication of the temple. Of David.

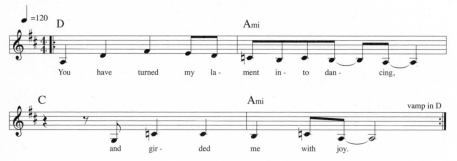

1     I will exalt you, O God,
        because you have lifted me up
        and have not let my enemies triumph over me.
2     O God, my God,
        I cried out to you,
        and you restored me to health.
3     You brought me up, O God, from the dead;
        you restored my life as I was going down to the grave.

**antiphon**

4 Sing to God, you servants;
      give thanks for the remembrance of holiness.
5 For God's wrath endures but the twinkling of an eye,
      God's favor for a lifetime.
  Weeping may spend the night,
      but joy comes in the morning.

**antiphon**

6 While I felt secure,
      I said, "I shall never be disturbed.
7    You, God, with your favor,
      made me as strong as the mountains."
  Then you hid your face,
      and I was filled with fear.
8 I cried to you, O God;
      I pleaded with God, saying,
9    "What profit is there in my blood,
      if I go down to the Pit?
  Will the dust praise you?
  Will it declare your faithfulness?
10 Hear, O God, and have mercy upon me;
      O God, be my helper."

**antiphon**

11 You have turned my wailing into dancing;
      you have put off my sack-cloth and clothed me with joy.
12 Therefore my heart sings to you without ceasing;
      O God my God, I will give you thanks forever.

**antiphon**

*Despite its superscript, which connects this psalm with the dedication of the temple, this prayer probably originated as a thanksgiving for recovery from illness (recovery from illness is often equated with being brought up from the dead in ancient Near Eastern literature). Although the fifth verse is probably the most famous, I was drawn to the eleventh; church life is full of singing and praising, but we could probably stand a bit more dancing.*

## 31  To the leader. A Psalm of David.

In - to your hand I en - trust my spi - rit. Ran - som me, God, my faith - ful Lord.

I have be - come like a bro - ken ves - sel, I am for - got - ten as though I were dead.

1    In you, O God, have I taken refuge;
        let me never be put to shame;
        deliver me in your righteousness.

2    Incline your ear to me;
        make haste to deliver me.

3    Be my strong rock,
        a castle to keep me safe.
    You are my crag and my stronghold;
        for the sake of your Name, lead me and guide me.

4    Take me out of the net that they have secretly set for me,
        for you are my tower of strength.

5    Into your hands I commend my spirit,
        for you have redeemed me, O God, O God of truth.

6    I hate those who cling to worthless idols,
        and I put my trust in God.

7    I will rejoice and be glad because of your mercy;
        for you have seen my affliction;
        you know my distress.

8    You have not shut me up in the power of the enemy;
        you have set my feet in an open place.

**antiphon**

9    Have mercy on me, O God,
        for I am in trouble;
        my eye is consumed with sorrow,
        and also my throat and my belly.

10   For my life is wasted with grief,
        and my years with sighing;
        my strength fails me because of affliction,
        and my bones are consumed.

11  I have become a reproach to all my enemies and
        even to my neighbors,
        a dismay to those of my acquaintance;
        when they see me in the street they avoid me.
12  I am forgotten like a dead man, out of mind;
        I am as useless as a broken pot.
13  For I have heard the whispering of the crowd;
        fear is all around;
        they put their heads together against me;
        they plot to take my life.

**antiphon**

14  But as for me, I have trusted in you, O God.
        I have said, "You are my God."
15  My times are in your hand;
        rescue me from the hand of my enemies and pursuers,
16  Make your face to shine upon your servant,
        and in your loving-kindness save me.
17  God, let me not be ashamed for having called upon you;
        rather, let the wicked be put to shame;
        let them be silent in the grave.
18      Let the lying lips be silenced
        which speak against the righteous,
        haughtily, disdainfully, and with contempt.

**antiphon**

19  How great is your goodness, O God!
        which you have laid up for those who fear you;
        which you have done in the sight of all
        for those who put their trust in you.
20  You hide them in the covert of your presence
        from those who slander them;
        you keep them in your shelter
        from the strife of tongues.
21  Blessed be God!
        who has shown me the wonders of love
        in a besieged city.

22  Yet I said in my alarm,
> "I have been thrust from your sight."
> Yet you heard the sound of my entreaty
> when I cried out to you.

23  Love God, all you who worship;
> God protects the faithful,
> but fully repays
> those who act haughtily.

24  Be strong and let your heart take courage,
> all you who wait for God.

**antiphon**

*In addition to being quoted by Jesus on the cross, this psalm is notable for its frequent alternation between trust, petition, and lament. Unlike many psalms, it doesn't build from lament to petition to trust but rather moves back and forth between them. I tried to squeeze all three sentiments into the antiphon, while still writing something that would be useable on Good Friday, when this psalm is most commonly read.*

## 32   Of David. A Maskil.

Show me which way to go, Coun - sel me with your eye up - on me.

1   Happy are they whose transgressions are forgiven,
> and whose sin is put away!

2   Happy are they to whom God imputes no guilt,
> and in whose spirit there is no guile!

**antiphon**

3   While I held my tongue,
> my bones withered away,
> because of my groaning all day long.

4   For your hand was heavy upon me
> day and night;
> my moisture was dried up as
> in the heat of summer.
> Then I acknowledged my sin to you,
> and did not conceal my guilt.

5    I said, "I will confess my transgressions to God."
     Then you forgave me the guilt of my sin.
6    Therefore all the faithful will make their prayers to you
         in time of trouble;
         when the great waters overflow,
         they shall not reach them.
7    You are my hiding-place;
         you preserve me from trouble;
         you surround me with shouts of deliverance.

**antiphon**

8    "I will instruct you
         and teach you in the way that you should go;
         I will guide you with my eye.
9    Do not be like horse or mule, which have no understanding;
         who must be fitted with bit and bridle,
         or else they will not stay near you."
10   Great are the tribulations of the wicked;
         but mercy embraces
         those who trust in God.
11   Be glad, you righteous, and rejoice in God;
         shout for joy, all who are true of heart.

**antiphon**

*Here we have the second Penitential Psalm (the first was Psalm 6), although at times it seems like a wisdom psalm and at other times like a psalm of thanksgiving. Rather than ending with admission of guilt, the psalm follows confession with forgiveness, and then counsel and penitence, just like the Sacrament of Penitence. Finally, it ends with an invitation to praise and be joyful.*

**33**

Let your con- stant love sur - round us, as we put our trust in you.

Let your con- stant love sur - round us, as we put our trust in you.

1    Rejoice in God, you righteous;
        it is good for the just to sing praises.

2    Praise God with the harp;
        play upon the psaltery and lyre.

3    Sing a new song;
        play sweetly with shouts of joy.

4    For the word of God is right,
        and all God's works are sure.

5    God loves righteousness and justice;
        the loving-kindness of God fills the whole earth.

6    By the word of God were the heavens made,
        by the breath of God's mouth all the heavenly hosts.

7    God gathers up the waters of the ocean as in a water-skin
        and stores up the depths of the sea.

**antiphon**

8    Let all the earth fear God;
        let all who dwell in the world stand in awe.

9    For God spoke, and it came to pass;
        God commanded, and it stood fast.

10   God brings the will of the nations to naught;
        and thwarts the designs of the peoples.

11   But God's will stands fast forever,
        and the designs of God's heart from age to age.

**antiphon**

12   Happy is the nation whose God is God!
        happy the people chosen to be God's own!

13  God looks down from heaven,
        and beholds all the people in the world.
14  God sits enthroned he gazes
        on all who dwell on the earth.
15        God fashions all the hearts of them
        and understands all their works.

**antiphon**

16  There is no ruler who can be saved by a mighty army;
        a strong person is not delivered by great strength.
17        The horse is a vain hope for deliverance;
        for all its strength it cannot save.
18  Behold, the eye of God is upon those who fear,
        on those who wait upon love,
19        To pluck their lives from death,
        and to feed them in time of famine.
20   We set our hope in God,
        who is our help and our shield.
21        Indeed, our heart rejoices,
        for in the holy Name we put our trust.
22  Let your loving-kindness, O God, be upon us,
        as we have put our trust in you.

**antiphon**

*The psalms aren't arranged randomly; whoever compiled the Psalter put a lot of thought into it. Perhaps in response to the invitation to praise at the end of Psalm 32, Psalm 33 happens to be a psalm of praise, one of the few that we find in the first two books of the Psalter. This particular psalm hearkens back to the "thesis statement" of Psalm 2 and foreshadows the emphasis on praise that we'll find toward the end of the Psalter.*

## 34  Of David, when he feigned madness before Abimelech, so that he drove him out, and he went away.

1   I will bless God at all times;
>  praise shall ever be in my mouth.
2   I will glory in God;
>  let the humble hear and rejoice.
3   Proclaim with me the greatness of God;
>  let us exalt the Name together.

**antiphon**

4   I sought God, who answered me
>  and delivered me out of all my terror.
5   Look upon God and be radiant,
>  and let not your faces be ashamed.
6   I called in my affliction
>  and God heard me
>  and saved me from all my troubles.
7   The angel of God encompasses those who fear,
>  and will deliver them.
8   Taste and see that God is good;
>  happy are they who trust!
9   Fear God, you that are saints,
>  for those who fear lack nothing.
10  The young lions lack and suffer hunger,
>  but those who seek God lack nothing that is good.

**antiphon**

11  Come, children, and listen to me;
>  I will teach you the fear of God.

12 Who among you loves life
      and desires long life to enjoy prosperity?
13 Keep your tongue from evil-speaking
      and your lips from lying words.
14 Turn from evil and do good;
      seek peace and pursue it.

**antiphon**

15 The eyes of God are upon the righteous,
      the ears of God are open to their cry.
16 The face of God is against those who do evil,
      to root out the remembrance of them from the earth.
17 The righteous cry, and God hears them
      and delivers them from all their troubles.
18 God is near to the brokenhearted
      and will save those whose spirits are crushed.
19 Many are the troubles of the righteous,
      but God will deliver them out of them all.
20 God will keep safe all their bones;
      not one of them shall be broken.
21 Evil shall slay the wicked,
      and those who hate the righteous will be punished.
22 God ransoms the life of servants,
      and none will be punished who trust.

**antiphon**

    *This is another acrostic psalm like Psalms 9 and 17, and it seems didactic in origin: "Come, children, listen to me; I will teach you the way of God." The superscription, incidentally, is in error: David pretended to be insane to Achish, not Abimelech (1 Samuel 21).*

## 35    Of David.

Then my soul will re - joice in you. Then I shall praise you in the con - gre - ga - tion.

Then my tongue will tell of your jus - tice all day long, all day long.

1    Fight those who fight me, O God;
     attack those who are attacking me.
2    Take up shield and armor
     and rise up to help me.
3    Draw the sword and bar the way
     against those who pursue me;
     tell me, "I am your salvation."
4    Let those who seek after my life
     be shamed and humbled;
     let those who plot my ruin
     fall back and be dismayed.
5    Let them be like chaff before the wind,
     and let the angel of God drive them away.
6    Let their way be dark and slippery,
     and let the angel of God pursue them.

**antiphon**

7    For they have secretly spread a net for me without a cause;
     without a cause they have dug a pit to take me alive.
8    Let ruin come upon them unawares;
     let them be caught in the net they hid;
     let them fall into the pit they dug.
9    Then I will be joyful in God;
     I will glory in his victory.
10   My very bones will say,
     "God, who is like you?
     You deliver the poor from those who are too strong for them,
     the poor and needy from those who rob them."

**antiphon**

11  Malicious witnesses rise up against me;
      they charge me with matters I know nothing about.
12  They pay me evil in exchange for good;
      I am full of despair.
13  But when they were sick
      I dressed in sack-cloth
      and humbled myself by fasting.
      I prayed with my whole heart.
14  As one would for a friend or a brother;
      I bowed down
      like one who mourns for a mother,
15  But when I stumbled, they were glad and gathered together;
      they gathered against me;
      strangers whom I did not know
      tore me to pieces and would not stop.
16  They put me to the test and mocked me;
      they gnashed at me with their teeth.

**antiphon**

17  O God, how long will you look on?
    Rescue me from the roaring beasts,
      and my life from the young lions.
18      I will give you thanks in the great congregation;
      I will praise you in the mighty throng.
19  Do not let my treacherous foes rejoice over me,
      nor let those who hate me without cause wink at each other.
20  For they do not plan for peace,
      but invent deceitful schemes against the quiet in the land.
21  They opened their mouths at me
      and said, "Aha! We saw it with our own eyes."

**antiphon**

22  You saw it, O God;
      do not be silent;
    O God, be not far from me.
23  Awake, arise to my cause!
      to my defense, my God and my God!
24  Give me justice, O God, my God, according to your righteousness;
      do not let them triumph over me.

25  Do not let them say in their hearts,
        "Aha! Just what we want!"
        Do not let them say,
        "We have swallowed that one up."
26  Let all who rejoice at my ruin
        be ashamed and disgraced;
        let those who boast against me
        be clothed with dismay and shame.
27  Let those who favor my cause
        sing out with joy and be glad;
        let them say always,
        "Great is God,
        who desires the prosperity of the servant."
28      And my tongue shall be talking of your righteousness
        and of your praise all the day long.

**antiphon**

*Most psalms of lament end with a promise of praise, but this one has three separate promises of praise (vv. 9–10, 18, and 28) spaced throughout the psalm, with stanzas of complaint and petition scattered between. I turned the threefold promise into a threefold antiphon.*

## 36    To the leader. Of David, the servant of God.

1   There is a voice of rebellion deep in the hearts of the wicked;
        there is no fear of God before their eyes.
2       They flatter themselves in their own eyes
        that their hateful sin will not be found out.

3   The words of their mouths are wicked and deceitful;
        they have left off acting wisely and doing good.
4   They think up wickedness upon their beds
        and set themselves in no good way;
        they do not abhor that which is evil.

**antiphon**

5   Your love, O God, reaches to the heavens,
        and your faithfulness to the clouds.
6       Your righteousness is like the strong mountains,
        your justice like the great deep;
        you save both people and beasts, O God.
7   How priceless is your love, O God!
    Your people take refuge under the shadow of your wings.
8   They feast upon the abundance of your house;
        you give them drink from the river of your delights.
9   For with you is the well of life,
        and in your light we see light.
10  Continue your loving-kindness to those who know you,
        and your favor to those who are true of heart.
11  Let not the foot of the proud come near me,
        nor the hand of the wicked push me aside.
12  See how they are fallen, those who work wickedness,
        cast down and unable to rise.

**antiphon**

*The word for "feast" here, יִרְוְיֻן, is the same word that is translated as "overflows" in the 23rd Psalm. It conveys a sense of overwhelming abundance. With the food and drink imagery, this would work very nicely as a table blessing or an invitation to communion.*

*Although this psalm is used in the lectionary, the verse about "he thinks of mischief in bed" is unfortunately omitted.*

## 37 Of David.

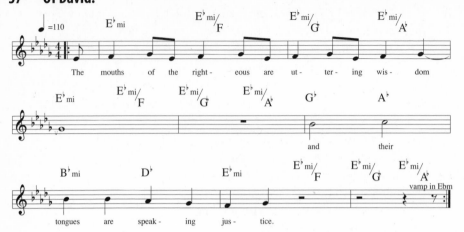

The mouths of the right - eous are ut - ter - ing wis - dom

and their

tongues are speak - ing jus - tice.

1 Do not fret yourself because of evildoers;
   do not be jealous of those who do wrong.
2 For they shall soon wither like the grass,
   and like the green grass fade away.
3 Put your trust in God and do good;
   dwell in the land and feed on its riches.
4 Take delight in God,
   who shall give you your heart's desire.
5 Commit your way to God
   and put your trust in God, who will bring it to pass.
6 God will make your righteousness as clear as the light
   and your just dealing as the noonday.
7 Be still and wait patiently before God
   Do not fret yourself over the one who prospers,
   the one who succeeds in evil schemes.

**antiphon**

8 Refrain from anger, leave rage alone;
   do not fret yourself;
   it leads only to evil.
9 For evildoers shall be cut off,
   but those who wait upon God
   shall possess the land.
10 In a little while the wicked shall be no more;
   you shall search out their place,
   but they will not be there.

11   But the lowly shall possess the land;
          they will delight in abundance of peace.

**antiphon**

12   The wicked plot against the righteous
          and gnash at them with their teeth.
13   God laughs at the wicked,
          and sees that their day will come.
14   The wicked draw their sword and bend their bow
          to strike down the poor and needy,
          to slaughter the upright.
15   Their sword shall go through their own heart,
          and their bow shall be broken.
16   The little that the righteous has
          is better than great riches of the wicked.
17   For the power of the wicked shall be broken,
          but God upholds the righteous.

**antiphon**

18   God cares for the lives of the godly,
          and their inheritance shall last forever.
19        They shall not be ashamed in bad times,
          and in days of famine they shall have enough.
20   As for the wicked, they shall perish,
          and the enemies of God shall vanish;
          like meadow grass consumed in smoke.
21   The wicked borrow and do not repay,
          but the righteous are generous in giving.

**antiphon**

22   Those who are blessed by God shall possess the land,
          but those who are cursed by God shall be destroyed.
23   Their steps are made firm by God,
          when God delights in their way.
24   If they stumble, they shall not fall headlong,
          for God holds them by the hand.
25   I have been young and now I am old,
          but never have I seen the righteous forsaken,
          or their children begging bread.

26  The righteous are always generous in their lending,
        and their children shall be a blessing.

**antiphon**

27  Turn from evil, and do good,
        and dwell in the land forever.
28  For God loves justice;
        he does not forsake his faithful ones.
    They shall be kept safe forever,
        but the offspring of the wicked shall be destroyed.
29  The righteous shall possess the land
        and dwell in it forever.
30  The mouth of the righteous utters wisdom,
        and their tongue speaks what is right.
31  The law of their God is in their heart,
        and their footsteps shall not falter.
32  The wicked spy on the righteous
        and seek occasion to kill them.
33      God will not abandon them to their hand,
        nor let them be found guilty when brought to trial.

**antiphon**

34  Wait upon God and keep the way;
        God will raise you up to possess the land,
        and when the wicked are cut off, you will see it.
35  I have seen the wicked in their arrogance,
        flourishing like a tree in full leaf.
36  I went by, and behold, they were not there;
        I searched for them, but they could not be found.

**antiphon**

37  Mark those who are honest; observe the upright;
        for there is a future for the peaceable.
38  Transgressors shall be destroyed, one and all;
        the future of the wicked is cut off.
39  But the deliverance of the righteous comes from God,
        who is their stronghold in time of trouble.

40   God will help them and rescue them;
        and will rescue them from the wicked and deliver them,
        because they seek refuge.

**antiphon**

*This is a wisdom psalm, and it uses much of the same language as other wisdom literature, like Proverbs, especially in the comparison of the righteous to the wicked. I like how the parallelism of verse 30 implies that justice is the natural extension of wisdom.*

## 38   A Psalm of David, for the memorial offering.

1   O God, do not rebuke me in your anger;
        do not punish me in your wrath.
2   For your arrows have already pierced me,
        and your hand presses hard upon me.
3   There is no health in my flesh because of your rage;
        there is no soundness in my body, because of my sin.
4   For my iniquities overwhelm me;
        like a heavy burden they are too much for me to bear.
5   My wounds stink and fester
        because of my foolishness.
6   I am bent and bowed;
        I go about in mourning all the day long.
7   My loins are filled with searing pain;
        there is no health in my body.
8   I am utterly numb and crushed;
        I wail, because of the groaning of my heart.

**antiphon**

9   O God, you know all my desires,
        and my sighing is not hidden from you.
10  My heart is pounding,
        my strength has failed me,
        and the brightness of my eyes is gone from me.

11  My friends and companions draw back from my affliction;
        my neighbors stand afar off.
12  Those who seek after my life lay snares for me;
        those who strive to hurt me speak of my ruin
        and plot treachery all the day long.
13  But I am like the deaf who do not hear,
        like those who are mute and who cannot speak.
14  I have become like one who does not hear
        from whose mouth comes no defense.

**antiphon**

15  For in you, O God, have I fixed my hope;
        you will answer me, O God, my God.
16  For I said, "Do not let them rejoice at my expense,
        those who gloat over me when my foot slips."
17  I am on the verge of falling,
        and my pain is always with me.
18  I will confess my iniquity
        and be sorry for my sin.
19  My enemies are mighty,
        my treacherous foes are many.
20  Those who repay evil for good
        slander me because I follow the course that is right.

**antiphon**

21  O God, do not forsake me;
        be not far from me, O my God.
22  Make haste to help me,
        O God of my salvation.

**antiphon**

*This is the third Penitential Psalm, and it begins with the exact same words as the first one, Psalm 6. For those communities who find the three-part antiphon from Psalm 6 to be intimidating, this antiphon would work for either psalm.*

## 39    To the leader: to Jeduthun. A Psalm of David.

1   I said, "I will keep watch upon my ways,
        so that I do not offend with my tongue.
        I will put a muzzle on my mouth
        while the wicked are in my presence."

2   So I held my tongue, silent;
        I was still
        but my pain became unbearable.

3   My heart was hot within me;
        my thoughts were flames;
        I spoke out with my tongue:

4    God, let me know my end and the number of my days,
        so that I may know how short my life is.

5   You have given me a mere handful of days,
        and my lifetime is as nothing in your sight;
        truly, we are but a puff of wind.

6   We walk about like a shadow,
        and in vain we are in turmoil;
        we heap up riches and cannot tell who will gather them.


**antiphon**

7    And now, what is my hope?
        O God, my hope is in you.

8    Deliver me from all my transgressions
        and do not make me the taunt of the fool.

9    I fell silent and did not open my mouth,
        for surely it was you that did it.

10   Take your affliction from me;
        I am worn down by the blows of your hand.

11   With rebukes for sin you punish us;
            like a moth you eat away all that is dear to us.
            We are but a puff of wind.

**antiphon**

12   Hear my prayer, O God,
            and give ear to my cry;
            hold not your peace at my tears.
            For I am but a sojourner with you,
            a wayfarer, as all my forebears were.
13   Turn your gaze from me, that I may be glad again,
            before I go my way and am no more.

**antiphon**

   *Two things struck me here. First, verses 4–6 remind me of Ecclesiastes, and I imag-
ine the psalmist at the end of his or her life, looking back on the accomplishments of a
lifetime and wondering if it will have any lasting effect. I was also taken by the first verse,
which seems to echo the Epistle of James in its emphasis of sins of the tongue. I once heard
John Bell say that the Bible is much more interested in condemning malicious gossip than
just about any other sin.*

## 40   To the leader. Of David. A Psalm.

You are my help and my res - cue - er.   My God,   do not de - lay.

1   I waited patiently upon God;
            who stooped to me
            and heard my cry.
2   God lifted me out of the desolate pit,
            out of the mire and clay
            and set my feet upon a high cliff,
            making my footing sure.
3   God put a new song in my mouth,
            a song of praise to our God.
      Many shall see, and stand in awe,
            and put their trust in God.

4    Happy are they who trust in God!
          they do not turn to the proud or turn the false.

**antiphon**

5    Great things are they that you have done, O God, my God!
          How great your wonders and your plans for us!
          There is none who can be compared with you.
          Oh, that I could make them known and tell them,
          but they are more than I can count.
6    You have led me to believe
          in sacrifice and offering you take no pleasure;
          burnt-offering and sin-offering you have not required.
7    So I said, "Behold, I come.
          It is written in the roll of the book concerning me:
8    'I love to do your will, O my God;
          your law is deep in my heart.'"
9    I proclaimed righteousness in the great congregation;
          behold, I did not restrain my lips;
          and that, O God, you know.
10   I have not hidden your righteousness in my heart;
          I have spoken of your faithful deliverance;
          I have not concealed your faithful love from the great congregation.
11   You are God; do not withhold your compassion from me;
          let your faithful love keep me safe forever.

**antiphon**

12   For innumerable troubles have crowded upon me;
          my sins have overtaken me,
          I cannot see;
          they are more than the hairs of my head,
          and my heart fails me.
13   Be pleased, O God, to deliver me;
          O God, make haste to help me.
14   Let them who seek after my life to destroy it
          be ashamed and altogether dismayed.
          Let them who take pleasure in my misfortune
          draw back and be disgraced.
15   Let those who say "Aha!" and gloat over me
          be confounded, because they are ashamed.

16    Let all who seek you rejoice in you and be glad;
      let those who love your salvation continually say, "Great is God!"
17  Though I am poor and afflicted,
      God will have regard for me.
      You are my helper and my deliverer;
      do not tarry, O my God.

**antiphon**

    *If you haven't checked out the U2 song "40," go buy it. No, seriously, go download an MP3 and come back after you've listened to it. Those guys do more with two chords than most people can do with a dozen. I tried to pay homage to that song with this antiphon, and I wrote it with the same basic shape. I encourage you to try using the chorus from "40" as an alternative antiphon for this psalm—it works pretty well.*

    *Also note that you can use the antiphon from Psalm 70 for the last five verses, if you want. They work well together.*

## 41    For the leader. A Psalm of David.

1    Blessed are they who consider the poor and needy!
      God will deliver them in the time of trouble.
2    God preserves them and keeps them alive,
        so that they may be happy in the land;
      They are not subject to the will of their enemies.
3    God sustains them on their sickbed
        and ministers to them in their illness.
4    I said, "God, be merciful to me;
        heal me, for I have sinned against you."
5    My enemies say wicked things about me,
        wondering when I will die and my name perish.
6    Even if they come to see me, they speak empty words;
        their heart collects false rumors;
        they go outside and spread them.

7   All my enemies whisper together about me
        and devise evil against me.
8   They say that a deadly thing has fastened on me,
        that I have taken to my bed and will never get up again.

**antiphon**

9   Even my best friend, whom I trusted,
        who broke bread with me,
        has lifted the heel and turned against me.
10  But you, O God, be merciful to me.
        Raise me up and I shall repay them.
11  By this I know you are pleased with me,
        that my enemy does not triumph over me.
12  In my integrity you hold me fast,
        and shall set me before your face forever.

**antiphon**

13  Blessed be the Most High, God of Israel,
        from age to age.
        Amen. Amen.

**antiphon**

*I'm not sure if Jesus was quoting Psalm 41 when he delivered the Beatitudes, but I kind of think he was. (Note that the Greek* makarios, *the Latin* beatus, *and the Hebrew* 'ashrey (אַשְׁרֵי) *can all be translated either as "happy" or "blessed.") Matthew says "Blessed are the poor in spirit" while Luke says "Blessed are the poor," and many people comment on the fact that Matthew spiritualizes Luke's message about poverty. Maybe Psalm 41 provides a middle ground—"Blessed are they who consider the poor and needy." This is the take that j. Snodgrass and I used when writing our song on the Beatitudes (from Trans-mission), and its themes resonate very strongly with those of the psalm.*

# Book II

## 42    To the leader. A Maskil of the Korahites.

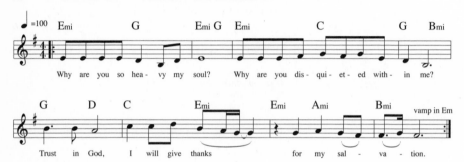

1    As the deer longs for the water-brooks,
         my entire being cries for you, O God.
2         My soul thirsts for God, for the living God;
         when shall I come to appear before your presence?
3    My tears have been my food day and night,
         while all day long they say to me, "Where now is your God?"
4    I pour out my spirit when I think on these things;
         how I went with the multitude,
         a festive crowd, into the house of God
         with the joyful shouts.
5    Why are you so full of heaviness, O my soul?
         and why are you so disquieted within me?
    Put your trust in God;
         for I will yet give thanks to the one
         who is my salvation and my God.

**antiphon**

6   My soul is heavy within me;
        therefore I will remember you
        from the land of Jordan and Hermon,
        and from the peak of Mizar,
7       where deep calls to deep
        in the noise of your cataracts;
        all your rapids and floods have swept over me.
8   God grants loving-kindness in the daytime;
        in the night season a song is with me,
        a prayer to the God of my life.
9   I will say to God, my rock,
        "Why have you forgotten me?
        and why do I go so heavily
        while the enemy oppresses me?"
10  While my bones are being broken,
        my enemies mock me to my face;
        All day long they mock me: "Where is your God?"
11  Why are you so full of heaviness, O my soul?
        and why are you so disquieted within me?
        Put your trust in God;
        for I will yet give thanks to the one
        who is my salvation and my God.

## antiphon

 *This psalm, and the one that follows it, were pretty clearly written as a single psalm. This is obvious for at least three reasons: First, the two psalms, when combined, follow the archetypical lament structure of complaint (42:1–10), petition (43:1), profession of trust (43:2–3), and promise of praise (43:4). Reading one psalm without the other only gives half the picture. Second, although Psalm 42 has a superscription, Psalm 43 doesn't, which is unusual in this part of the Psalter, but makes sense if it's the second half of 42. Finally, the two psalms share an antiphon in 42:5, 42:11, and 43:5.*

 *The antiphon itself serves as a microcosm of the entire psalm. First you have the complaint (Why are you heavy my soul? Why are you disquieted within me?), then a profession of trust (Trust in God), and finally a promise of praise (I will give thanks for my salvation). Because this antiphon is original and fits the psalms so well (and because I want to discourage anyone from using one psalm without the other), I've written just one antiphon for both.*

**43**

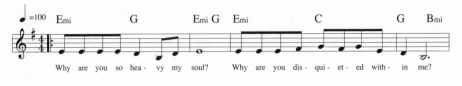

Why are you so hea-vy my soul? Why are you dis-qui-et-ed with-in me?

Trust in God, I will give thanks for my sal - va - tion.

1   Give judgment for me, O God,
    and defend my cause
    against an ungodly people;
    deliver me from the deceitful and the wicked.

2   For you are the God of my strength;
    why have you put me from you?
    Why do I go so heavily
    while the enemy oppresses me?

3   Send out your light and your truth,
    that they may lead me,
    and bring me to your holy hill
    and to your dwelling;

4   That I may go to the altar of God,
    God, my joy and gladness,
    on the harp I will give thanks to you,
    O God, my God.

**antiphon**

5   Why are you so full of heaviness, O my soul?
    and why are you so disquieted within me?
    Put your trust in God;
    for I will yet give thanks to the one
    who is my salvation and my God.

**antiphon**

*Christian translators often default to translating the word ישׁוּעֹת (yeshuot) as salvation, but it can mean a lot of other things, including welfare, prosperity, victory, and deliverance. The BCP and the NRSV translate it here as "help" while the JPS translates it as "saving presence."*

*Interestingly, Yeshuah is also Hebrew for "Jesus" and is much closer to what he was probably called in his native Aramaic. This, combined with the fact that these psalms are used during the Easter vigil, led me to choose "salvation," but with the full knowledge that this is not the only interpretation. Note that I would never suggest that the original psalmist was prophetically referring to Jesus; for one thing, the word here is plural, giving us "I will give thanks for my Jesuses."*

## 44 To the leader. Of the Korahites. A Maskit.

1  We have heard with our ears, O God,
      our ancestors have told us,
      the deeds you did in their days,
      in the days of old.
2  How with your hand you drove the peoples out
      and planted our ancestors in the land;
      how you destroyed nations
      and made your people flourish.
3  For they did not take the land by their sword,
      nor did their arm win the victory for them;
      but your right hand, your arm, and the light of your countenance,
      because you favored them.
4  You are my Sovereign and my God;
      you command victories for Jacob.
5  Through you we gore our foes;
      through your Name we trampled our enemies.
6  For I do not rely on my bow,
      and my sword does not give me the victory.
7  Surely, you gave us victory over our adversaries
      and put those who hate us to shame.
8  Every day we gloried in God,
      and we will praise your Name forever.

**antiphon**

9   Nevertheless, you have rejected and humbled us
        and do not go forth with our armies.
10  You have made us fall back before our adversary,
        and our enemies have plundered us.
11  You have made us like sheep to be eaten
        and have scattered us among the nations.
12  You are selling your people for a trifle
        and are making no profit on the sale of them.
13  You have made us the scorn of our neighbors,
        a mockery and derision to those around us.
14  You have made us a byword among the nations,
        a laughing-stock among the peoples.
15  My humiliation is daily before me,
        and shame has covered my face
16      because of the taunts of the mockers and blasphemers,
        because of the enemy and avenger.

**antiphon**

17  All this has come upon us;
        yet we have not forgotten you,
        nor have we betrayed your covenant.
18  Our heart never turned back,
        nor did our footsteps stray from your path;
19      Though you thrust us down into a place of misery,
        and covered us over with deep darkness.
20  If we have forgotten the Name of our God,
        or stretched out our hands to some strange god,
21      will not God, who knows the secrets of the heart,
        find it out?
22  Indeed, for your sake we are killed all the day long;
        we are accounted as sheep for the slaughter.

**antiphon**

23  Awake, O God! why are you sleeping?
    Arise! Do not reject us forever!
24  Why have you hidden your face
        and forgotten our affliction and oppression?
25  We sink down into the dust;
        our body cleaves to the ground.

26 Rise up, and help us,
      and save us, for the sake of your steadfast love.

**antiphon**

*We have another use of the word* Yeshuah, *this time in the form of "my sword will not save me," although many translators render it "my sword will not give me victory." In today's world, it's important to remember that the way of Jesus, which can save us, is an alternative to the way of the sword, which cannot. As Tertullian said in the second century, "In disarming Peter [in Gethsemane], Christ disarmed all Christians."*

## 45    To the leader: according to the Lilies. Of the Korahites. A Maskil. A love song.

1   My heart is stirring with a noble song;
      let me recite what I have fashioned for the king;
      my tongue shall be the pen of a skilled writer.

**antiphon**

2   You are the fairest of men;
      grace flows from your lips,
      because God has blessed you forever.
3   Strap your sword upon your thigh, O mighty warrior,
      in your pride and in your majesty.
4   Ride out and conquer in the cause of truth
      and for the sake of justice.
      Your right hand will show you marvelous things;
5   Your arrows are very sharp, O mighty warrior.
      The peoples are falling at your feet,
      and the king's enemies are losing heart.
6   Your throne, O God, endures forever and ever,
      your royal scepter is a scepter of equity.
7   You love righteousness and hate iniquity.
      Therefore God, your God, has anointed you
      with the oil of gladness above your fellows.

8    All your garments are fragrant with
         myrrh, aloes, and cassia,
         and the music of strings
         from ivory palaces makes you glad.
9    Kings' daughters stand among the ladies of the court;
         on your right hand is the queen,
         adorned with the gold of Ophir.

**antiphon**

10   "Hear, O daughter; consider
         and listen closely;
         forget your people and your father's house.
11       The king will have pleasure in your beauty;
         he is your master; therefore do him honor.
12   The people of Tyre are here with a gift;
         the rich among the people seek your favor."

**antiphon**

13   All glorious is the princess as she enters;
         her gown is cloth-of-gold.
14       In embroidered apparel she is brought to the king;
         after her the bridesmaids follow in procession.
15   With joy and gladness they are brought,
         and enter into the palace of the king.
16   "In place of fathers, O king, you shall have sons;
         you shall make them princes over all the earth.

**antiphon**

17   I will make your name to be remembered for all generations;
         therefore nations will praise you forever and ever."

**antiphon**

    *On the whole, the Bible doesn't have much to say about romantic love. Anyone who's ever tried to pick readings or hymns for a wedding knows that it's really difficult! Other than the Song of Songs, this psalm is as close as we get to a love song and, indeed, the lectionary puts the two texts together on Proper 17b. Psalm 45 doesn't have the mutuality or innocence of the Songs of Songs, though, and rather than the giddy thoughts of two secret lovers, we're given an official song written by a court scribe for a royal wedding. As love songs go, this one's kind of nerdy.*

## 46    To the leader. Of the Korahites. According to Alamoth. A Song.

1    God is our refuge and strength,
        a very present help in trouble.
2    Therefore we will not fear,
        though the earth moves,
        and though the mountains topple into the depths of the sea;
3        its waters rage and foam,
        and mountains tremble at its tumult.

**antiphon**

4    There is a river whose streams gladden the city of God,
        the holy habitation of the Most High.
5    God is in the midst of her; she shall not be overthrown;
        God shall help her at the break of day.
6    The nations rage, and the kingdoms are shaken;
        God has spoken, and the earth shall melt away.
7    The God of hosts is with us;
        the God of Jacob is our stronghold.

**antiphon**

8    Come now and look upon the works of God,
        what awesome things God has done on earth.
9    God makes war to cease in all the world;
        God breaks the bow, shatters the spear,
        and burns the shields with fire.
10    "Be still, then, and know that I am God;
        I will be exalted among the nations;
        I will be exalted in the earth."
11    God of hosts is with us;
        the God of Jacob is our stronghold.

**antiphon**

*Verses 7 and 11 form a clear antiphon. If the refrain were also added after verse 3 (and 9b omitted), then the psalm would divide perfectly into three equal stanzas, each with three verses. Formal elements like this lend credence to the tradition that the Korahites were a guild of professional liturgists, as mentioned in 2 Chronicles 20.*

## 47   To the leader. Of the Korahites. A Psalm.

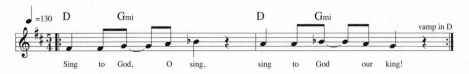

Sing to God, O sing, sing to God our king!

1   Clap your hands, all you peoples;
       shout to God with a cry of joy.
2   For God Most High is to be feared;
       a great ruler over all the earth.
3       God subdues the peoples under us,
       and the nations under our feet.
4   God chooses our inheritance for us,
       the pride of Jacob the beloved.

**antiphon**

5   God has gone up with a shout,
       God with the sound of the ram's-horn.
6   Sing praises to God, sing praises;
       sing praises to our ruler, sing praises.
7       For God is ruler of all the earth;
       sing a hymn.
8   God reigns over the nations;
       God sits upon a holy throne.
9   The nobles of the peoples have gathered together
       with the people of the God of Abraham.
       The rulers of the earth belong to God,
       who is highly exalted.

**antiphon**

At this point you've probably noticed that a lot of the psalms in this part of the Psalter are attributed to the Korahites, a group of poets and musicians during the monarchial period of Israel's history. Since the Korahites were funded by the king, their psalms are very nationalistic and very pro-monarchy, in contrast to some other psalms that claim that God favors the poor over the powerful. This psalm is no exception and contains very militaristic, imperial imagery, especially verses 3–4, which place all other nations as subjects at the feet of Israel. By the end of the psalm, however, a more universal tone is reached, implying that all nations have a place in God's retinue.

The Korahite psalms are very poetic, clearly written by professionals. The verse for this antiphon reads:

| | |
|---|---|
| Zamru Elohim, zameru | זַמְּרוּ אֱלֹהִים זַמֵּרוּ; |
| Zamru lemalkenu zameru | זַמְּרוּ לְמַלְכֵּנוּ זַמֵּרוּ |

I tried to capture the musicality and rhythm of this psalm.

## 48    A Song. A Psalm of the Korahites.

1    Great is God, and highly to be praised;
    in the city of our God
    is the holy hill.

2    Beautiful and lofty, the joy of all the earth,
    is the hill of Zion,
    the very center of the world
    city of the great Sovereign.

3    God is in her citadels
    and is known to be her sure refuge.

4    Behold, the rulers of the earth assembled
    and marched forward together.

5    They looked and were astounded;
    they retreated and fled in terror.

6    Trembling seized them there;
    they writhed like a woman in childbirth,

7    like ships of Tarshish
    when the east wind shatters them.

8    As we have heard, so have we seen,
    in the city of God of hosts,
    in the city of our God;
    God has established her forever.

9   We have waited in silence on your loving-kindness, O God,
        in the midst of your temple.
10  Your praise, like your Name, O God,
        reaches to the world's end;
        your right hand is full of justice.
11  Let Mount Zion be glad!
    Let the cities of Judah rejoice,
        because of your judgments.

**antiphon**

12  Make the circuit of Zion;
        walk round about her;
        count her towers.
13      Consider well her bulwarks;
        examine her strongholds;
        that you may tell those who come after.
14  This God is our God forever and ever,
        our guide for evermore.

**antiphon**

*Having no real connection to Zion or to Jerusalem, many Christians have histori-cally imagined that passages like this refer to the church. Reading psalms in this way can be useful, even it doesn't accurately reflect the psalmist's intent.*

*The final word here is traditionally translated as "forever" or "evermore," but the actual Hebrew is עַל-מוּת, literally "over death." The word before it, יְנַהֲגֵנוּ, is the same word that's used for driving a chariot or a herd of sheep. So instead of "God will guide us forevermore," it could be translated "God will drive us over death."*

*In New York City, many churches are closing or being combined; the Catholic church closed a dozen parishes last year and the Lutheran church is considering doing something similar. Many fear that the church is dying, but I don't believe it. The church of the future might look different than the church of the past, but God will drive us to where we need to be, and we will get to tell the next generation all about it.*

## 49  To the leader. Of the Korahites. A Psalm.

1  Hear this, all you peoples;
       hearken, all you who dwell in the world,
2      you of high degree and low,
       rich and poor together.
3  My mouth shall speak of wisdom,
       and my heart is full of insight.
4  I will incline my ear to a proverb
       and set forth my riddle upon the harp.

**antiphon**

5  Why should I be afraid in evil days,
       when the wickedness of those at my heels surrounds me,
6      those who put their trust in their wealth,
       and boast of their great riches?
7  We can never ransom ourselves,
       or deliver to God the price of our life,
8      for the ransom of our life is great,
       and can never be enough.

9  In order to live forever and ever,
       and never see the grave.

**antiphon**

10  For we see that the wise die also;
        like the dull and stupid they perish
        and leave their wealth to those who come after them.
11  Their graves shall be their homes forever,
        their dwelling places from generation to generation,
        though they call the lands after their own names.
12  Even though honored, they cannot live forever;
        they are like the beasts that perish.

**antiphon**

105

13 Such is the way of those who foolishly trust in themselves,
and the end of those who delight in their own words.

**antiphon**

14 Like a flock of sheep they are destined to die;
Death is their shepherd;
they go down straightway to the grave.
Their form shall waste away,
and the land of the dead shall be their home.
15 But God will ransom my life;
and will snatch me from the grasp of death.

**antiphon**

16 Do not be envious when some become rich,
or when the grandeur of their houses increase;
17 For they will carry nothing away at their death,
nor will their grandeur follow them.
18 Though they thought highly of themselves while they lived,
and were praised for their success,
19 They shall join the company of their ancestors,
who will never see the light again.
20 Those who are honored, but have no understanding,
are like the beasts that perish.

**antiphon**

*Here, of course, we have an exception to our usual Korahite expectations. Rather than focusing on the king, God's anointed one, or Zion, God's favored nation, the psalmist focuses on impermanence of material things, much like Ecclesiastes, one of my favorite books in the Bible.*

## 50    A Psalm of Asaph.

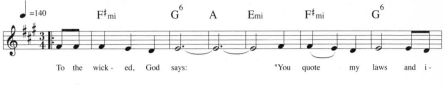

To the wick - ed, God says:    "You quote    my laws    and i -

mag - ine    I'm    just    like    you."

1    God, the God of gods, has spoken;
  and has called the earth
  from the rising of the sun to its setting.
2    Out of Zion, perfect in its beauty,
  God shines in glory.
3     Our God will come and will not keep silence;
 Before God there is consuming flame,
  and round about a raging storm.
4    God calls the heavens and the earth from above
  to witness the judgment of the people.
5    "Gather before me my loyal followers,
  those who made a covenant with me with a sacrifice."
6    Let the heavens declare the rightness of God's cause;
  for God is judge.

**antiphon**

7    Hear, O my people, and I will speak:
  "O Israel, I will bear witness against you;
 I am God, your God.
8    I do not accuse you because of your sacrifices;
  your offerings are always before me.
9     I will take no bull-calf from your stalls,
  nor he-goats out of your pens;
10    For all the beasts of the forest are mine,
  the herds in their thousands upon the hills.
11    I know every bird in the sky,
  and the creatures of the fields are in my sight.
12    If I were hungry, I would not tell you,
  for the whole world is mine and all that is in it.

13  Do you think I eat the flesh of bulls,
        or drink the blood of goats?
14  Offer to God a sacrifice of thanksgiving
        and make good your vows to the Most High.
15  Call upon me in the day of trouble;
        I will deliver you, and you shall honor me."


**antiphon**


16  But to the wicked God says:
        "Why do you recite my statutes,
        and take my covenant upon your lips;
17      Since you refuse discipline,
        and toss my words behind your back?
18  When you see a thief, you make him your friend,
        and you cast in your lot with adulterers.
19      You have loosed your lips for evil,
        and harnessed your tongue to a lie.
20      You are always speaking evil of your brother
        and slandering your own mother's son.
21  These things you have done, and I kept still,
        and you thought that I am like you."
        But I have made my accusation and lay a charge before you.
22  Consider this well, you who forget God,
        lest I rend you and there be none to deliver you.


**antiphon**


23  "Whoever offers me the sacrifice of thanksgiving honors me;
        but to those who keep in my way
        I will show the salvation of God."


**antiphon**


*Even in the ancient times, the psalmist recognized that worship could be insincere and that people can faithfully go through the motions of worship without actually following God's will. Voltaire wrote, "If God has made us in his image, we have returned him the favor," and that is the sin of which the wicked are accused in this psalm. It's a temptation that we all must be on guard against, especially those of us in the emergent church who fancy ourselves to be pioneers and reformers.*

## 51   To the leader. A Psalm of David, when the prophet Nathan came to him, after he had gone in to Bathsheba.

O - pen my lips and my mouth will de - clare your praise.

1   Have mercy on me, O God,
        according to your loving-kindness;
        in your great compassion
        blot out my offenses.
2   Wash me through and through from my wickedness
        and cleanse me from my sin
3        for I know my transgressions,
        and my sin is ever before me.
4   Against you only have I sinned
        and done what is evil in your sight,
        so you are justified when you speak
        and upright in your judgment.
5   Indeed, I have been wicked from my birth,
        a sinner from my mother's womb.
6   For behold, you look for truth deep within me,
        and will teach me secret wisdom.

**antiphon**

7   Purge me from my sin, and I shall be pure;
        wash me, and I shall be clean indeed.
8   Make me hear of joy and gladness,
        that the body you have broken may rejoice.
9   Hide your face from my sins
        and blot out all my iniquities.
10  Create in me a clean heart, O God,
        and renew a right spirit within me.
11  Cast me not away from your presence
        and take not your holy Spirit from me.
12  Give me the joy of your saving help again
        and sustain me with your bountiful Spirit.
13  I shall teach your ways to the wicked,
        and sinners shall return to you.

antiphon

14   Deliver me from death,
          O God, O God of my salvation.
          and my tongue shall sing of your righteousness,
15   Open my lips, O God,
          and my mouth shall proclaim your praise.
16   Had you desired it, I would have offered sacrifice,
          but you take no delight in burnt-offerings.
17   The sacrifice of God is a troubled spirit;
          O God, you will not despise
          a broken and contrite heart.

antiphon

18   Be favorable and gracious to Zion,
          and rebuild the walls of Jerusalem.
19   Then you will be pleased with the appointed sacrifices,
          with burnt-offerings and oblations;
          then shall they offer young bullocks upon your altar.

antiphon

*Psalm 51 is quite famous, and is used most often on Ash Wednesday. The fifteenth verse is used to open matins in the liturgy of the hours and morning prayer in the Episcopal tradition. If you don't know the story of David and Bathsheba (2 Samuel 11), it's a wonderful story of temptation, penitence, and a prophet courageous enough to speak truth to power. This is also the fourth Penitential Psalm.*

## 52   To the leader. A Maskil of David, when Doeg the Edomite came to Saul and said to him, "David has come to the house of Ahimelech."

1   You tyrant, why do you boast of wickedness against the godly?
          All day long you plot ruin;
2   Your tongue is like a sharpened razor,
          O worker of deception.

3   You love evil more than good
        and lying more than speaking the truth.
4   You love all words that hurt,
        O you deceitful tongue.
5   Oh, that God would demolish you utterly,
        topple you, and snatch you from your dwelling,
        and root you out of the land of the living!
6   The righteous shall see and tremble,
        and they shall laugh you, saying,
7       "This is the one who did not take God for a refuge,
        but trusted in great wealth
        and relied upon wickedness."

**antiphon**

8   But I am like a green olive tree in the house of God;
        I trust in the mercy of God forever and ever.
9   I will give you thanks for what you have done
        and declare the goodness of your Name
        in the presence of the godly.

**antiphon**

*The "mighty one" is presumably King Saul (1 Samuel 22), about to be uprooted from the Temple (and God's favor) in order to be supplanted by David. We also get more admonishments against valuing wealth too highly; we should ground ourselves in God instead.*

## 53  To the leader: according to Mahalath. A Maskil of David.

1   The fool has said in his heart,
     "There is no God."
    All are corrupt and commit abominable acts;
     there are none who do any good.

2   God looks down from heaven upon us all,
     to see if there are any who are wise,
     if there is one who seeks after God.

3   Every one has proved faithless;
     all alike have turned bad;
     there are none who do good;
     no, not one.

4   Have they no knowledge, those evildoers
     who eat up my people like bread
     and do not call upon God?

5   See how greatly they tremble,
     such trembling as never was;
     for God has scattered the bones of the enemy;
     they are put to shame,
     because God has rejected them.

**antiphon**

6   Oh, that Israel's deliverance would come out of Zion!
     when God restores the fortunes of his people
     Jacob will rejoice and Israel be glad.

**antiphon**

*With the exception of one verse, this is the exactly the same as Psalm 14. This antiphon uses a slightly more hopeful text than the one I chose for Psalm 14; congregations can use either antiphon, depending on their mood, or the two can be sung together as counterpoint.*

*Interested folks should check out how Paul uses these psalms in Romans 3.*

## 54   To the leader: with stringed instruments. A Maskil of David, when the Ziphites went and told Saul, "David is in hiding among us."

You are my help-er, the sus-tain-er of my life.

1   Save me, O God, by your Name;
       in your might, defend my cause.
2   Hear my prayer, O God;
       give ear to the words of my mouth.
3   For the arrogant have risen up against me,
       and the ruthless have sought my life,
       those who have no regard for God.

**antiphon**

4   But God is my helper;
       it is God who sustains my life.
5   Render evil to those who spy on me;
       in your faithfulness, destroy them.
6   I will offer you a freewill sacrifice
       and praise your Name, O God, for it is good,
7       for you have rescued me from every trouble,
       and my eye has seen the ruin of my foes.

**antiphon**

*The word "helper," עֵזֶר, is the same word used in Genesis 2 when God decides to make a "helpmeet" for Adam; this word is also applied to God in Psalms 10, 30, and 72. In fact, this word is almost always used to refer to God. If one uses Genesis to show that women should be subservient to men, therefore, it follows from Psalm 54 that God should be subservient to humanity. I don't believe either.*

## 55   To the leader: with stringed instruments. A Maskil of David.

It is not an en - e - my who taunts me, it is not a foe who stands a - gainst me,

it is you my com - pan - ion, my friend.

1   Hear my prayer, O God;
    do not hide yourself from my petition.
2   Listen to me and answer me.
    I have no peace, because of my cares.
3   I am shaken by the noise of the enemy
    and by the oppression of the wicked,
    for they bring evil upon me
    and are set against me in fury.
4   My heart quakes within me,
    and the terrors of death have fallen upon me.
5   Fear and trembling have come over me,
    and horror overwhelms me.
6   And I said,
    "Oh, that I had wings like a dove!
    I would fly away and be at rest.
7   I would flee to a far-off place
    and make my lodging in the wilderness.
8   I would hasten to escape
    from the stormy wind and tempest."

**antiphon**

9   Confuse them, O God; confound their speech;
    For I have seen violence and strife in the city.
10  Day and night the watchmen make their rounds upon her walls,
    but trouble and misery are in the midst of her.
11  There is corruption at her heart;
    her streets are never free of oppression and deceit.

**antiphon**

12  For had it been an adversary who taunted me,
        then I could have borne it;
        or had it been an enemy who vaunted himself against me,
        then I could have hidden.
13   But it was you, one after my own heart,
        my companion, my own familiar friend.
14   Our friendship was sweet;
        we walked together in the house of God.
15  Let death come upon them suddenly;
        let them go down alive to the grave;
    For where they dwell
        is evil.

**antiphon**

16  But I will call upon God,
        and God will deliver me.
17  Evening, morning, and noonday,
        I will complain and lament,
        and God will hear my voice.
18  God will bring me safely back
        from the battle waged against me;
        for there are many who fight me.
19  God, who is enthroned of old,
        will hear me and bring them down;
        they never change;
        they do not fear God.

**antiphon**

20  My companion hurt a friend;
        and broke a covenant
21      with speech softer than butter,
        but war is in his heart,
        with words smoother than oil,
        but they are drawn swords.

**antiphon**

22  Cast your burden upon God, who will sustain you;
        who will never let the righteous stumble.

23  For you will bring the bloodthirsty and deceitful
        down to the pit of destruction, O God.
        They shall not live out half their days,
        but I will put my trust in you.

**antiphon**

*Although this psalm changes voice several times, it is heartbreakingly personal. Although it's certainly been used for acts of public worship (and verses 9–11 might have been added for that purpose), I have little doubt that there was some specific betrayal of trust that led someone to write this psalm.*

## 56    To the leader: according to The Dove on Far-off Terebinths. Of David. A Miktam, when the Philistines seized him in Gath.

In God whose word I praise.    I will not be a-fraid.
Put my tears in-to your bot-tle.    Put my fears in-to your book.

1    Have mercy on me, O God,
        for my enemies are hounding me;
        all day long they assault and oppress me.
2    They hound me all the day long;
        many are my adversaries, O Most High.
3    When I am afraid, I will put my trust in you.
4        In God, whose word I praise,
        in God I trust.
        I will not be afraid,
        for what can mortals do to me?
5    All day long they damage my cause;
        their only thought is to do me evil.
6    They band together; they lie in wait;
        they spy upon my footsteps, seeking my life.
7    Shall they escape despite their wickedness?
        O God, in your anger, cast down the peoples.

**antiphon**

8    You have noted my lamentation;
         put my tears into your bottle;
         are they not recorded in your book?
9    Whenever I call upon you, my enemies will be put to flight;
         this I know, for God is on my side.
10   In God, whose word I praise,
         in God, whose word I praise,
11       in God I trust.
         I am not afraid,
         for what can mortals do to me?
12   I am bound by the vow I made to you, O God;
         I will present to you thank-offerings;
13   For you have rescued me from death,
         my feet from stumbling,
         that I may walk before God in the light of the living.

**antiphon**

*I love the imagery of putting your tears into God's bottle for safekeeping, but this tune has an embedded antiphon in verses 4 and 10–11. I felt like I ought to use that antiphon, but I'm adding in the alternate lyrics just in case you want to use them.*

## 57   To the leader: Do Not Destroy. Of Dave.
##      A Miktam, when he fled from Saul, in the cave.

1    Be merciful to me, O God, be merciful,
         for I have taken refuge in you;
         in the shadow of your wings will I take refuge
         until danger has gone by.
2    I will call upon the Most High God,
         the God who is good to me.
3    God will send from heaven and save me;
         God will send forth faithful love.
         and will confound those who trample upon me;

**antiphon**

4    I lie in the midst of man-eating lions;
        their teeth are spears and arrows,
        their tongue a sharp sword.
5    Exalt yourself above the heavens, O God,
        and your glory over all the earth.
6    They have laid a net for my feet, and I am bowed low;
        they have dug a pit before me,
        but have fallen into it themselves.

**antiphon**

7    My heart is firm, O God,
        my heart is firm;
        I will sing and make melody.
8    Wake up, my spirit!
        Awake, lute and harp!
        I will wake the dawn.
9    I will confess you among the peoples, O God;
        I will sing praise to you among the nations.
10    For your loving-kindness is greater than the heavens,
        and your faithfulness reaches to the clouds.
11  Exalt yourself above the heavens, O God,
        and your glory over all the earth.

**antiphon**

*This is a classic individual lament, supposedly reflecting the events of 1 Samuel 22–24. The psalm contains the record of an antiphon in verses 5 and 11, although it's not clear to me whether those verses were part of the original composition. The words of the embedded antiphon don't really convey a sense of lament, so I made the music quite dark to compensate.*

## 58   To the leader: Do Not Destroy. Of David. A Miktam.

Ru - lers, what do you de - cree? Do you judge with e - qui - ty?

1  Do you indeed decree righteousness, you rulers?
   Do you judge the peoples with equity?
2  No, you devise evil in your hearts,
     and your hands deal out violence in the land.
3  The wicked are perverse from the womb;
     liars go astray from their birth.
4  They are as venomous as a serpent,
     a deaf adder which stops its ears,
5     which does not heed the voice of the charmer,
     no matter how skillful his charming.

**antiphon**

6  O God, break their teeth in their mouths;
     pull the fangs of the young lions, O God.
7  Let them vanish like water that runs off;
     let them wither like trodden grass.
8  Let them be like the snail that melts away;
     like a stillborn child that never sees the sun.
9  Before they bear fruit, let them be cut down like a brier;
     let them be swept away like thorns and thistles.

**antiphon**

10  The righteous will be glad when they see the vengeance;
     they will bathe their feet in the blood of the wicked.
11  And they will say,
     "Surely, there is a reward for the righteous;
     surely, there is a God who rules in the earth."

**antiphon**

*Psalms don't get much angrier than this. I must chime in and disagree with the psalmist regarding one thing: I don't think anyone is wicked from the day they're born.*

119

## 59    To the leader: Do Not Destroy. Of David. A Miktam, when Saul ordered his house to be watched in order to kill him.

I sing to you. You are my strength and ha - ven.

They run a - round ev - ery night like snar - ling dogs!

1    Rescue me from my enemies, O God;
         protect me from those who rise up against me.
2    Rescue me from evildoers
         and save me from those who thirst for my blood.
3    See how they lie in wait for my life,
         how the mighty gather together against me;
         for no offense of mine,
         for no fault of mine, O God,
4        for no guilt of mine,
         they run and prepare themselves for battle.
      Rouse yourself, come to my side, and see.
5    You, Most High, God of hosts,
         God of Israel.
         Awake, and punish all the ungodly;
         show no mercy to those who are faithless and evil.

**antiphon**

6    They go to and fro in the evening;
         they snarl like dogs and run about the city.
7    Behold, they boast with their mouths,
         and taunts are on their lips;
         "Who hears us?" they say.
8    But you, O God, you laugh at them;
         you laugh all the ungodly to scorn.

**antiphon**

9    My eyes are fixed on you, O my Strength;
         for you, O God, are my haven.
10   My merciful God comes to meet me;
         God will let me look in triumph on my enemies.

11 Do not slay them, O God, lest my people forget;
    send them reeling by your might
    and put them down, O God our shield,
12    for the sins of their mouths,
    for the words of their lips,
 Let them be caught in their pride.
    for the cursing and lies that they utter.
13 Make an end of them in your wrath;
    make an end of them, and they shall be no more.
    Let everyone know that God rules in Jacob,
    and to the ends of the earth.

**antiphon**

14 They go to and fro in the evening;
    they snarl like dogs and run about the city.
15 They forage for food,
    and if they are not filled, they howl.
16 For my part, I will sing of your strength;
    I will celebrate your love in the morning;
    For you have become my haven,
    a refuge in the day of my trouble.

**antiphon**

17 To you, O my Strength, will I sing;
    for you, O God, are my haven and my merciful God.

**antiphon**

*There are actually two antiphons in this text, which is unusual. The top one comes from verses 9 and 17, and the bottom come from verses 6 and 14. For those who are interested, scholars think that the words "Do Not Destroy" probably refer to a melody that can be used with more than one set of words, just like* Slane, Picardy, *or* Hyfrydol *can be used for many different hymns.*

## 60 To the leader: according to the Lily of the Covenant. A Miktam to David; for instruction; when he struggled with Aram-naharaim and with Aram-zobah, and when Joab on his return killed twelve thousand Edomites in the Valley of Salt.

1   O God, you have cast us off
        You have broken us;
        You have been angry;
        Restore us!
2   You have shaken the earth
        and split it open;
    Repair the cracks in it,
        for it totters.
3   You have made your people know hardship;
        you have given us wine that makes us stagger.
4   You have set up a banner for those who fear you,
        to be a refuge from the power of the bow.
5   Save us by your right hand and answer us,
        that those who are dear to you may be delivered.

**antiphon**

6   God spoke from the holy place and said:
        "I will exult and parcel out Shechem;
        I will divide the valley of Succoth.
7       Gilead is mine and Manasseh is mine;
        Ephraim is my helmet,
        Judah my scepter.

8       Moab is my washbasin,
         on Edom I throw down my sandal,
         and over Philistia will I shout in triumph."

**antiphon**

9      Who will lead me into the strong city?
        Who will bring me to Edom?

**antiphon**

10  Have you not cast us off, O God?
        you no longer march, O God, with our armies.
11  Grant us your help against the enemy,
        for vain is the help of mortals.
12  With God we will do valiant deeds,
        and trample our enemies under foot.

**antiphon**

*The traditional view credits this psalm to David, claiming that it recounts the wars he fights in 2 Samuel 8–10. It's interesting that the book of Samuel depicts David as confident and mighty, gloriously driving his enemies to flee before him, while this psalm depicts a much more desperate and fearful voice. Personally, I think the psalm is a more accurate representation of the prayers of terrified soldiers.*

## 61   To the leader: with stringed instruments. Of David.

Let me a-bide in your tent for-ev-er.

1      Hear my cry, O God,
        and listen to my prayer.
2   I call upon you from the ends of the earth
        with heaviness in my heart;
        set me upon the rock that is higher than I.
3   For you have been my refuge,
        a strong tower against the enemy.

4    I will dwell in your house forever;
        I will take refuge under the cover of your wings.

**antiphon**

5    For you, O God, have heard my vows;
        you have granted me the heritage of those who fear your Name.
6    Add length of days to the king's life;
        and years extending over many generations.
7        Let the king sit enthroned before God forever;
        appoint love and faithfulness for protection.
8    So will I always sing the praise of your Name,
        and day by day I will fulfill my vows.

**antiphon**

*Although this psalm has the form of a lament, its words are surprisingly hopeful as
the psalmist prays for long life. If you believe the attribution to David, then when he prays
for long life for the king, he's actually praying for himself, and the psalm as a whole makes
a bit more sense.*

## 62    To the leader: according to Jeduthun. A Psalm of David.

1    For God alone I wait in silence;
        from whom comes my salvation.
2    God alone is my rock and my salvation,
        my stronghold; I shall not be shaken.
3    How long will you assail me
            to crush me, all of you together,
            as if you were a leaning fence, a toppling wall?
4    They seek only to bring me down from my place of honor;
            lies are their chief delight.
            They bless with their lips,
            but in their hearts they curse.

**antiphon**

5    For God alone I wait in silence;
        truly, my hope is in God.
6    God alone is my rock and my salvation,
        my stronghold; I shall not be shaken.
7    In God is my safety and my honor;
        my rock of strength;
        my refuge.
8    Put your trust in God always, O people,
        pour out your hearts,
        for God is our refuge.

**antiphon**

9    Those of high degree are mere breath,
        those of low estate are an illusion.
        On the scales together
        they are lighter than a breath,
10   Put no trust in extortion;
        in robbery take no empty pride;
        if wealth increases, set not your heart upon it.
11   God has spoken once,
        twice have I heard it,
        that power belongs to God.
12   Steadfast love is yours, O God,
        for you repay everyone according to deeds.

**antiphon**

*The antiphon in this psalm is in verses 1–2 and 5–6. Being a twentysomething in New York City, my life tends to be loud, busy, and stressful. Studies have shown that Americans work more and sleep less than we did a century ago, and taking a moment to wait for God in silence can be really difficult to squeeze into a day. It's important, though.*

*It's hard to write a song about silence (unless you're Simon and Garfunkel), so I wrote something really simple and sparse that could be sung over a drone on the notes E and B. The empty space at the end of the antiphon is important—don't skip it! Extremely musical communities might want to try singing it as a round at one measure, which gives it a gentle rise and fall, but results in some crunchy harmonies. You can also sing it as a round at the second measure, giving it a nice call-and-response feel which works well a capella.*

## 63    A Psalm of David, when he was in the Wilderness of Judah.

1    O God, you are my God;
      I seek you;
      my soul thirsts for you,
      my flesh yearns for you,
      as in a parched and thirsty land that has no water.
2    Therefore I have gazed upon you in your holy place,
      that I might behold your power and your glory.
3    For your loving-kindness is better than life itself;
      my lips shall give you praise.
4    So will I bless you as long as I live
      and lift up my hands in your Name.
5    I am content, as with marrow and fatness,
      and my mouth praises you with joyful lips,
6      when I remember you upon my bed,
      and meditate on you in the night watches.
7    For you have been my helper.
      I will rejoice
      under the shadow of your wings.
8    My entire being clings to you;
      your right hand holds me fast.

**antiphon**

9    May those who seek my life to destroy it
      go down into the depths of the earth;
10   Let them fall upon the edge of the sword,
      and let them be food for jackals.
11   But the ruler will rejoice in God;
      all those who swear by God will be glad;
      for the mouths of liars shall be stopped.

**antiphon**

*This antiphon was improvised during a Transmission service led by Sarah Godbe-here, our resident dancer and choreographer. The word we translate as "my body," בְּשָׂרִי, is actually the word for flesh, and is the same word used in Psalm 50:13 ("Do I eat the flesh of bulls or drink the blood of goats?") as well as Genesis 2:24 ("Hence a man clings to his wife, so that they become one flesh"). This psalm reflects a very physical, embodied, and sensual sort of spirituality.*

## 64    To the leader. A Psalm of David

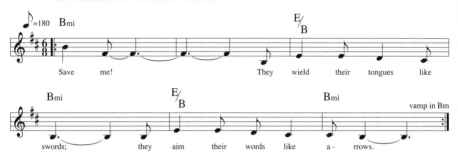

1    Hear my voice, O God, when I complain;
    protect my life from fear of the enemy.
2    Hide me from the conspiracy of the wicked,
    from the mob of evildoers.
3    They sharpen their tongue like a sword,
    and aim their bitter words like arrows,
4        that they may shoot down the blameless from ambush;
    they shoot without warning and are not afraid.
5    They hold fast to their evil course;
    they plan how they may hide their snares.
    They say, "Who will see us?
6    Who will find out our crimes?
    We have thought out a perfect plot.
    for the human mind and heart are a mystery."

**antiphon**

7    God will loose an arrow at them,
    and suddenly they will be wounded.
8    God will make them trip over their tongues,
    and all who see them will shake their heads.
9    Everyone will stand in awe
    and declare God's deeds;
    they will recognize God's works.

10   The righteous will rejoice in God
       and put their trust in God,
       and all who are true of heart will glory.

**antiphon**

*Anyone who's ever felt unjustly slandered or gossiped about will understand this psalm immediately. Again, I think of James, my favorite epistle.*

## 65   To the leader. A Psalm of David. A Song.

The fields are clothed with grain,     the hills are burst - ing with song!

1   You are to be praised, O God, in Zion;
       to you vows are paid.
2   To you that hear prayer
       shall all flesh come,
3   Our sins are stronger than we are,
       but you will blot them out.
4   Happy are they whom you choose
       and draw to your courts to dwell there!
       they will be satisfied by the beauty of your house,
       your holy temple.

**antiphon**

5   Awesome things will you show us in your righteousness,
       O God of our salvation,
       O Hope of the ends of the earth
       and the distant seas.
6   You make fast the mountains by your power;
       you are girded with might.
7   You still the roaring of the seas,
       the roaring of their waves,
       and the clamor of the peoples.
8   Those who dwell at the ends of the earth will tremble at your marvelous signs;
       you make the dawn and the dusk to sing for joy.

9   You visit the earth and water it abundantly;
        you make it very plenteous;
        the river of God is full of water.
        You prepare the grain,
        for so you provide for the earth.
10  You drench the furrows
        and smooth out the ridges;
        You soften it with heavy rain
        and bless its growth.
11  You crown the year with your bounty,
        and your paths overflow with plenty.
12  The fields of the wilderness overflow,
        and the hills are clothed with joy.
13  The meadows are covered with flocks,
        the valleys cloaked with grain;
        let them sing and shout for joy.

**antiphon**

*I know that Thanksgiving isn't an "official" religious holiday, but the Christian litur-gical year lacks a good harvest festival. Try using this psalm around the dinner table this year as a grace before you stuff yourselves and watch football!*

## 66   To the leader. A Song. A Psalm.

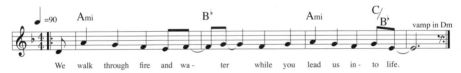

We walk through fire and wa - ter while you lead us in - to life.

1   Be joyful in God, all you lands;
2       sing the glory of the Name;
        sing the glory of praise.
3   Say to God,
        "How awesome are your deeds!
        because of your great strength enemies cringe before you.
4       All the earth bows down before you,
        sings hymns to you,
        sings out your Name."

**antiphon**

5    Come now and see the works of God,
>who does wonderful deeds toward all people.

6    God turned the sea into dry land,
>they crossed the water on foot,
>and there we rejoiced.

7    In might God rules forever;
>keeping watch over the nations;
>let no rebel rise up against God.

**antiphon**

8    Bless our God, you peoples;
>make the voice of praise be heard;

9    The one who grants us life
>will not allow our feet to slip.

**antiphon**

10   For you, O God, have proved us;
>you have tried us as silver is tried.

11   You brought us into the snare;
>you laid heavy burdens upon our backs.

12   You let enemies ride over our heads;
>we went through fire and water;
>but you brought us out into a place of refreshment.

**antiphon**

13   I will enter your house with burnt-offerings
>and will pay you my vows,

14   which I promised with my lips
>and spoke with my mouth in distress.

15   I will offer you sacrifices of fat beasts
>with the smoke of rams;
>I will give you oxen and goats.

**antiphon**

16   Come and listen, all you who fear God,
>and I will tell you what God has done for me.

17   I called out with my mouth,
>and praise was on my tongue.

18   If I had found evil in my heart,
         God would not have heard me;
19   But in truth God has heard me;
         and has attended to the voice of my prayer.
20   Blessed be God, who has not rejected my prayer,
         nor withheld love from me.

**antiphon**

*The way this psalm pairs a communal thanksgiving in the past tense (vv. 5–12) with a the personal thanksgiving in the present/future tense (vv. 13–20) makes it seem as if the trials endured are entirely in the past and the psalmist is now enjoying a life free of difficulty. Personally, I think that life can be difficult even once you begin dwelling in God's house and making offerings, so I put verse 12 into the present tense for the antiphon, a decision not supported by the Hebrew.*

*For an alternate antiphon, use the chorus from Joss Whedon's "Walk Through the Fire" from* Buffy the Vampire Slayer's *"Once More, with Feeling," which puts the fire-walking firmly in the present/future.*

## 67    To the leader: with stringed instruments. A Psalm. A Song.

1    May God be merciful to us and bless us,
         and may God's face shine upon us.
2        Let your ways be known upon earth,
         your deliverance among all nations.

**antiphon**

3    Let the peoples praise you, O God;
         all the peoples praise you.
4    Let the nations be glad and sing for joy,
         for you judge the peoples with equity
         and guide all the nations upon earth.
5    Let the peoples praise you, O God;
         let all the peoples praise you.

6   The earth has brought forth her increase;
        may God, our own God, give us a blessing.
7   May God give us a blessing,
        and may all the ends of the earth stand in awe.

**antiphon**

*The beginning of this psalm echoes the priestly benediction from Numbers 6: "May God bless you and keep you. May God make his face to shine upon you and be gracious to you. May God bestow favor upon you and give you peace." Although the above melody works just fine as an antiphon, you can also change the words from "us" to "you," split the congregation into two parts, and have them sing it to each other as a round. Doing this turns the antiphon into a benediction and is a lovely way to end a service.*

## 68   To the leader. Of David. A Psalm. A Song.

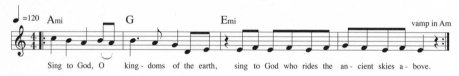

Sing to God, O king-doms of the earth, sing to God who rides the an-cient skies a-bove.

1   God will arise,
        let enemies be scattered;
        let those who hate God flee.
2   Let them vanish like smoke when the wind drives it away;
        as the wax melts at the fire,
        so let the wicked perish at the presence of God.
3   But let the righteous be glad and rejoice before God;
        let them also be merry and joyful.

**antiphon**

4   Sing to God, sing praises to the Name;
        exalt the one who rides upon the heavens;
        YHWH is the Name.
    Rejoice before God!
5       Guardian of orphans, defender of widows,
        God in the holy habitation!

6    God gives the solitary a home
        and brings forth prisoners into freedom;
        but the rebels shall live in dry places.

**antiphon**

7    O God, when you went forth before your people,
        when you marched through the wilderness,
8        the earth shook, and the skies poured down rain,
        at the presence of God, the God of Sinai,
        at the presence of God, the God of Israel.
9    You sent a gracious rain, O God, upon your inheritance;
        you refreshed the land when it was weary.
10   Your people dwell there;
        in your goodness, O God, you have made provision for the poor.

**antiphon**

11   God gave word;
        great was the company of women who bore the tidings:
12   "Generals with their armies are fleeing away;
        the women at home are dividing the spoils."
13   Though you lingered among the sheepfolds,
        a dove whose wings are covered with silver,
        whose feathers are fine gold.
14   When the Almighty scattered rulers,
        it was like snow falling in Zalmon.
15   O mighty mountain, O hill of Bashan!
        O rugged mountain, O hill of Bashan!
16   Why do you look with envy, O rugged mountain,
        at the hill which God chose for a resting place?
        God will dwell there forever.
17   The chariots of God are twenty thousand,
        thousands upon thousands;
        God comes in holiness from Sinai.

**antiphon**

18   You have gone up on high and led captives;
        you have received gifts
        even from your enemies,
        that the Most High God might dwell among them.

**antiphon**

19  Blessed be God
      who bears our burdens day by day,
      the God of our salvation.
20  Our God, the God of our salvation;
      God is Most High, by whom we escape death.
21  God shall crush the heads of enemies,
      and the hairy scalp of those who go on in their wickedness.
22  God has said, "I will bring them back from Bashan;
      I will bring them back from the depths of the sea;
23       That your foot may be dipped in blood,
      the tongues of your dogs in the blood of your enemies."

**antiphon**

24  They see your procession, O God,
      your procession, my God and my King,
      into the sanctuary.
25  The singers go before, musicians follow after,
      in the midst of maidens playing hand-drums.
26  Bless God in the congregation;
      bless God, you that are of the fountain of Israel.
27  There is Benjamin, least of the tribes, at the head;
      the princes of Judah in a company;
      and the princes of Zebulon and Naphtali.

**antiphon**

28  Send forth your strength, O God;
      establish, O God,
      what you have wrought for us,
      for your temple at Jerusalem.
29  Rulers shall bring gifts to you.
30  Rebuke the wild beast of the reeds,
      and the peoples, a herd of wild bulls with its calves.
      Trample down those who lust after silver.
Scatter the peoples that delight in war.
31  Let tribute be brought out of Egypt;
      let Cush stretch out her hands to God.

32  Sing to God,
      O kingdoms of the earth;
      sing praises to God
33      who rides in the heavens, the ancient heavens;
      who sends forth a voice, a mighty voice.
34  Ascribe power to God,
      whose majesty is over Israel;
      whose strength is in the skies.
35  How wonderful is God in holy places!
      the God of Israel giving strength and power to the people!
      Blessed be God!

**antiphon**

*This is one of the older psalms, and it uses a great deal of "heavenly warrior" imagery, including a storm-cloud chariot. This motif was common in other ancient Near Eastern religions. Check out Ephesians 4 to see a Christological interpretation by Paul.*

## 69   To the leader: according to Lilies. Of David.

1  Save me, O God,
      for the waters have risen up to my neck.
2  I am sinking in deep mire,
      and have no foothold
      I have come into deep waters,
      and the torrent washes over me.
3  I have grown weary with my crying;
      my throat is inflamed;
      my eyes have failed
      from looking for my God.

4    Those who hate me without a cause
        are more than the hairs of my head;
        those who would destroy me are mighty,
        my lying foes.
    Must I then give back what I never stole?

**antiphon**

5    O God, you know my foolishness,
        and my faults are not hidden from you.
6    Let not those who hope in you,
    Mighty God of hosts,
        be put to shame through me.
    Let not those who seek you,
    O God of Israel,
        be disgraced because of me.
7    Surely, for your sake have I suffered reproach,
        and shame has covered my face.
8    I have become a stranger to my own kindred,
        an alien to my mother's children.
9    Zeal for your house has eaten me up;
        the scorn of those who scorn you has fallen upon me.
10  I humbled myself with fasting,
        but that was turned to my reproach.
11  I put on sack-cloth also,
        and became a byword among them.
12  Those who sit at the gate murmur against me,
        and the drunkards make songs about me.

**antiphon**

13  But as for me, this is my prayer to you,
        at the time you have set, O God:
        "In your great mercy, O God,
        answer me with your unfailing help."
14  Save me from the mire;
        do not let me sink;
        let me be rescued from those who hate me
        and out of the deep waters.
15  Let not the torrent of waters wash over me,
        neither let the deep swallow me up;
        do not let the Pit shut its mouth upon me.

16    Answer me, O God,
            for your love is kind;
            in your great compassion, turn to me.
17    "Hide not your face from your servant;
            be swift and answer me, for I am in distress.
18    Draw near to me and redeem me;
            because of my enemies deliver me.

**antiphon**

19    You know my reproach,
            my shame, and my dishonor;
            my adversaries are all in your sight."
20    Reproach has broken my heart,
            and it cannot be healed;
            I looked for sympathy, but there was none,
            for comforters, but I find none.
21    They gave me gall to eat,
            vinegar to quench my thirst.

**antiphon**

22    Let the table before them be a trap
            and their sacred feasts a snare.
23    Let their eyes be darkened, that they may not see,
            and give them continual trembling in their loins.
24    Pour out your indignation upon them,
            and let the fierceness of your anger overtake them.
25        Let their camp be desolate,
            and let there be none to dwell in their tents.
26    For they persecute those whom you have stricken
            and add to the pain of those whom you have pierced.
27    Lay to their charge guilt upon guilt,
            and let them not receive your vindication.
28    Let them be wiped out of the book of the living
            and not be written among the righteous.

**antiphon**

29    As for me, I am afflicted and in pain;
            your help, O God, will lift me up on high.

30  I will praise the Name of God in song;
       I will proclaim God's greatness with thanksgiving.
31  This will please God more than an offering of oxen,
       more than bullocks with horns and hoofs.
32  The afflicted shall see and be glad;
       you who seek God, your heart shall live.
33  For God listens to the needy,
       and does not despise prisoners.
34  Let the heavens and the earth praise,
       the seas and all that moves in them;
35  For God will save Zion
       and rebuild the cities of Judah;
       they shall live there and possess it.
36  The children of servants will inherit it,
       and those who love God's Name will dwell therein.

**antiphon**

*The water imagery in the first three verses is really unique. Fans of Damien Rice should consider using "Cold Water" in conjunction with this psalm.*

## 70  To the leader. Of David, for the memorial offering.

1  Be pleased, O God, to deliver me;
       O God, make haste to help me.
2  Let those who seek my life
       be ashamed and altogether dismayed;
       let those who take pleasure in my misfortune
       draw back and be disgraced.
3  Let those who say to me "Aha!"
       turn back in frustration.

**antiphon**

4  Let all who seek you rejoice and be glad in you;
       let those who love your salvation say forever,
       "Great is God!"

5    But as for me, I am poor and needy;
         come to me speedily, O God.
     You are my helper and my deliverer;
         O God, do not tarry.

**antiphon**

This is just Psalm 40:13–17, with elohim *instead of YHWH. I used the same chords for this antiphon as I did for Psalm 40, and you can switch between them, if you want. It works well as AABB, with A being the fortieth antiphon and B being the seventieth antiphon.*

## 71

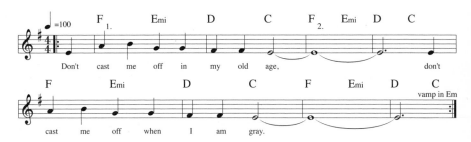

1    In you, O God, have I taken refuge;
         let me never be ashamed.
2    In your righteousness, deliver me and set me free;
         incline your ear to me and save me.
3    Be my strong rock, a castle to keep me safe;
         you are my crag and my stronghold.
4    Deliver me, my God, from the hand of the wicked,
         from the clutches of the evildoer and the oppressor.

**antiphon**

5    For you are my hope,
         O Most High God,
         my confidence since I was young.
6    I have been sustained by you ever since I was born;
         from my mother's womb you have been my strength;
         my praise shall be always of you.

7     I have become a portent to many;
> but you are my refuge and my strength.

8     Let my mouth be full of your praise
> and your glory all the day long.

9     Do not cast me off in my old age;
> forsake me not when my strength fails.

**antiphon**

10    For my enemies are talking against me,
> and those who lie in wait for my life take counsel together.

11    They say, "Pursue and seize that person
>> whom God has forsaken,
>> whom no one will save."

12    O God, be not far from me;
> come quickly to help me, O my God.

13    Let those who set themselves against me be put to shame and be disgraced;
> let those who seek to do me evil be covered with scorn and reproach.

**antiphon**

14    But I shall always wait in patience,
> and shall praise you more and more.

15    My mouth shall recount your mighty acts
> and saving deeds all day long;
> though I cannot know the number of them.

16    I will begin with the mighty works of Most High God;
> I will recall your righteousness, yours alone.

**antiphon**

17    O God, you have taught me since I was young,
> and to this day I tell of your wonderful works.

18    And now that I am old and gray-headed, O God, do not forsake me,
> till I make known your strength to this generation
> and your power to all who are to come.

19    Your righteousness, O God, reaches to the heavens;
> you have done great things.
> Who is like you, O God?

20    You have showed me great troubles and adversities,
> but you will restore my life
> and bring me up from the depths of the earth.

21  You strengthen me more and more;
       you enfold and comfort me,

**antiphon**

22  Therefore I will praise you upon the lyre
       for your faithfulness, O my God;
       I will sing to you with the harp,
       O Holy One of Israel.
23  My lips will sing with joy when I play to you,
       my whole being, which you have redeemed.
24  My tongue will proclaim your righteousness all day long,
       for they who sought to do me harm are ashamed and disgraced.

**antiphon**

*Loneliness and abandonment are two of the scariest things people face as they age. While visiting shut-ins I've heard people complain about feeling abandoned by their church and by their children; this psalmist feels abandoned by God. I find this psalm so heartbreaking that I wrote the antiphon as a two-part round—I wanted to make it clear to the congregation that they weren't singing alone.*

## 72  Of Solomon.

For he shall de-liv-er the poor who cry out in dis-tress, and
he shall have pi-ty on the need-y and the weak.

1  Give the King your justice, O God,
       and your righteousness to the King's son;
2      That he may rule your people righteously
       and the poor with justice.
3  That the mountains may bring prosperity to the people,
       and the little hills bring righteousness.
4  He shall defend the needy among the people;
       he shall rescue the poor
       and crush the oppressor.

5   He shall live as long as the sun and moon endure,
        from one generation to another.
6   He shall come down like rain upon the mown field,
        like showers that water the earth.
7       In his time shall the righteous flourish;
        there shall be abundance of peace
        till the moon shall be no more.

**antiphon**

8   He shall rule from sea to sea,
        and from the river to the ends of the earth.
9   His foes shall bow down before him,
        and his enemies lick the dust.
10  The kings of Tarshish and of the isles shall pay tribute,
        and the kings of Sheba and Saba offer gifts.
11  All kings shall bow down before him,
        and all the nations do him service.

**antiphon**

12  For he shall deliver the poor who cries out in distress,
        and the oppressed who has no helper.
13  He shall have pity on the lowly and poor;
        he shall preserve the lives of the needy.
14  He shall redeem their lives from oppression and violence,
        and dear shall their blood be in his sight.

**antiphon**

15  Long may he live, and receive gold from Sheba;
        may prayer be made for him always,
        and may they bless him all the day long.
16  May there be abundance of grain on the earth, to the tops of the mountains
        may its fruit flourish like Lebanon,
        and its grain like grass upon the earth.
17  May his name remain forever
        and be established as long as the sun endures;
        may all the nations bless themselves in him
        and call him blessed.

**antiphon**

18   Blessed be the Most High God, the God of Israel,
          who alone does wondrous deeds!
19   And blessed be God's glorious Name forever!
          and may all the earth be filled with glory.
          Amen. Amen.

**antiphon**

20   Here end the prayers of David son of Jesse.

**antiphon**

    *Although I do strive to use genderless language for God, this psalm is actually about the king and, if you believe the superscription, specifically about Solomon. According to the psalm, it is Solomon's duty to deliver the poor and needy and it is God's blessing that makes this possible. Unfortunately, Solomon didn't do too well when it came to taking care of the poor.*

# Book III

## 73   A Psalm of Asaph.

1   Truly, God is good to Israel,
        to those who are pure in heart.
2   But as for me, my feet had nearly slipped;
        I had almost tripped and fallen;
3       Because I envied the proud
        and saw the prosperity of the wicked:
4   Death had no pain for them,
        and their bodies are sleek and sound;
5   In the misfortunes of others they have no share;
        they are not afflicted as others are;
6   Therefore they wear their pride like a necklace
        and wrap violence about them like a cloak.
7   Their iniquity comes from gross minds,
        and their hearts overflow with wicked thoughts.
8   They scoff and speak maliciously;
        out of their haughtiness they plan oppression.
9   They set their mouths against the heavens,
        and their evil speech runs through the world.

**antiphon**

10   And so the people turn to them
        and find in them no fault.

11  They say, "How should God know?
        Is there knowledge in the Most High?"
12  So then, these are the wicked;
        always at ease, they increase their wealth.

**antiphon**

13  In vain have I kept my heart clean,
        and washed my hands in innocence.
14      I have been afflicted all day long,
        and punished every morning.
15  Had I gone on speaking this way,
        I should have betrayed the generation of your children.
16  When I tried to understand these things,
        it was too hard for me;
17  Until I entered the sanctuary of God
        and discerned the end of the wicked.

**antiphon**

18  Surely, you set them in slippery places;
        you cast them down in ruin.
19  Oh, how suddenly do they come to destruction,
        come to an end, and perish from terror!
20  Like a dream when one awakens, O God,
        when you arise you will make their image vanish.

**antiphon**

21  When my mind became embittered,
        I was sorely wounded in my heart.
22  I was stupid and had no understanding;
        I was like a brute beast in your presence.

**antiphon**

23  Yet I am always with you;
        you hold me by my right hand.
24  You will guide me by your counsel,
        and afterwards receive me with glory.
25  Whom have I in heaven but you?
        And, having you, I desire nothing upon earth.

26 Though my flesh and my heart should waste away,
   God is the strength of my heart and my portion forever.
27 Truly, those who forsake you will perish;
   you destroy all who are unfaithful.
28 But it is good for me to be near God;
   I have made the Most High God my refuge.
   I will speak of all your works.

**antiphon**

*The third book of Psalms starts off with eleven Psalms of Asaph, a Levite Temple musician mentioned in Chronicles. The Asaph Psalms are noteworthy for packing a lot more historical information than most. Asaph seemed to be aware of the creation, the exodus, the wandering in the desert, much of the problems that plagued the Davidic empire, and the destruction of the Temple at Shiloh.*

*This psalm is both a wisdom psalm, comparing the way of the wicked to the way of the righteous (like Proverbs), and an individual lament. The word translated as "prosperity" is שָׁלוֹם (Sh'lom), which could also be "complete" or "at ease," but I just couldn't pass up the alliteration of wicked, wanton, and wealthy.*

## 74    A Maskil of Asaph.

1 O God, why have you utterly cast us off?
   why is your wrath so hot against the sheep of your pasture?
2 Remember your congregation that you purchased long ago,
   the tribe you redeemed to be your inheritance,
   and Mount Zion where you dwell.

**antiphon**

3 Turn your steps toward the endless ruins;
   the enemy has laid waste everything in your sanctuary.
4 Your adversaries roared in your holy place;
   they set up their banners as tokens of victory.
5 They came with axes
   to a grove of trees;

6      they broke down all your carved work
         with hatchets and hammers.

7   They set fire to your holy place;
         they defiled and razed the dwelling-place of your Name.

8   They said to themselves, "Let us destroy them altogether."
         They burned down all the meeting-places of God in the land.

9   There are no signs for us to see;
         there is no prophet left;
         no one among us who knows how long.

**antiphon**

10  How long, O God, will the adversary scoff?
         will the enemy blaspheme your Name forever?

11  Why do you draw back your hand,
         your right hand hidden in your bosom?

**antiphon**

12  Yet God is my ruler from ancient times,
         victorious in the midst of the earth.

13     You divided the sea by your might
         and shattered the heads of the dragons upon the waters;

14     You crushed the heads of Leviathan
         and gave it to the people of the desert for food.

15     You split open spring and torrent;
         you dried up ever-flowing rivers.

16     Yours is the day, yours also the night;
         you established the moon and the sun.

17     You fixed all the boundaries of the earth;
         you made both summer and winter.

**antiphon**

18  Remember, O God, how the enemy scoffed,
         how a foolish people despised your Name.

19  Do not hand over the life of your dove to wild beasts;
         never forget the lives of your poor.

20  Look upon your covenant.
     The dark places of the earth are haunts of violence.

21  Let not the oppressed turn away ashamed;
         let the poor and needy praise your Name.

22 Arise, O God, maintain your cause;
       remember how fools revile you all day long.
23 Forget not the clamor of your adversaries,
       the unending tumult of those who rise up against you.

**antiphon**

*Just as Book II of the psalms begins with an individual lament (42–43) that is
followed up by a similar communal lament, so also does Book III and the Psalms of Asaph.
The antiphon is drawn from verse 21, but it's important to put it in the context of verse 20;
this is not a prayer on behalf of the poor, this is a prayer of the poor.*

## 75   To the leader: Do Not Destroy. A Psalm of Asaph. A Song.

1 We give you thanks, O God,
      we give you thanks,
      calling upon your Name
      and declaring all your wonderful deeds.

**antiphon**

2 "I will appoint a time,
      I will judge with equity.
3 Though the earth and all its inhabitants are quaking,
      I will make its pillars fast.
4 I will say to the boasters, 'Boast no more,'
      and to the wicked, 'Do not toss your horns;
5 Do not toss your horns so high,
      nor speak with a proud neck.'"
6 For judgment is neither from the east nor from the west,
      nor yet from the wilderness or the mountains.
7     It is God who judges,
      who puts down one and lifts up another.
8 For in God's hand there is a cup,
      full of spiced and foaming wine,
      pouring out,

and all the wicked of the earth shall drink
and drain the dregs.
9   But I will rejoice forever;
        I will sing praises to the God of Jacob.

**antiphon**

10  God shall break off all the horns of the wicked;
        but the horns of the righteous shall be exalted.

**antiphon**

*With the exception of the first verse, the psalmist uses the first person on behalf of God, like a prophet. I used the first verse lest anyone get confused.*

## 76   To the leader: Do Not Destroy. A Psalm of Asaph. A Song.

1   In Judah, God is known;
        God's Name is great in Israel.
2   At Salem is the tabernacle,
        and God's dwelling is in Zion.
3   There he broke the flashing arrows,
        the shield, the sword, and the weapons of war.

**antiphon**

4   How glorious you are,
        more splendid than the everlasting mountains!
5   The strong of heart have been despoiled;
        they sink into sleep;
        none of the warriors can lift a hand.

6 At your rebuke, O God of Jacob,
 both horse and rider lie stunned.
7 What terror you inspire!
 Who can stand before you
 when you are angry?
8 From heaven you pronounced judgment;
 the earth was afraid and was still;
9 when God rose up in judgment
 to save all the oppressed of the earth.

**antiphon**

10 Truly, wrathful Edom will give you thanks,
 and the remnant of Hamath will keep your feasts.
11 Make a vow to God, your God, and keep it;
 let all around bring gifts to the one who is worthy to be feared.
12 God breaks the spirit of princes,
 and strikes terror in the rulers of the earth.

**antiphon**

*This is another great psalm that never makes it into the lectionary. Aside from the imagery of God ruining weapons of war (perhaps in preparation for their being beaten into plowshares), it also locates this radical peacemaking in Salem, another name for Jerusalem. The Hebrew root* sh-l-m *means peace (or wholeness, or harmony), as in* Shalom, *and "Jerusalem" is often translated as "city of peace." How appropriate that the psalmist is proclaiming the breaking of instruments of violence in the city of peace!*

*Salem is the name the Torah uses to refer to Jerusalem (Genesis 14:18) when Melchizedek, acting as king of Salem and priest of God, blesses Abraham. Melchizedek, a rather mysterious figure, reappears in Psalm 110.*

## 77 To the leader: according to Jeduthun. Of Asaph. A Psalm.

I call to mind your deeds, re - mem - ber - ing your won - ders of old.

1 I will cry aloud to God;
 I will cry aloud, and God will hear me.
2 In the day of my trouble I sought God;
 my hands were stretched out by night

and did not tire;
    I refused to be comforted.
3   I think of God, I am restless,
    I ponder, and my spirit faints.

**antiphon**

4   You will not let my eyelids close;
    I am troubled and I cannot speak.
5   I consider the days of old;
    I remember the years long past;
6   I commune with my heart in the night;
    I ponder
    and search my mind.
7   Will God cast me off forever?
    Will God no more show me favor?
8   Has God's loving-kindness come to an end forever?
    Has God's promise failed for evermore?
9   Has God forgotten to be gracious?
    Has God, in anger, withheld compassion?
10  And I said, "My grief is this:
    the right hand of the Most High has lost its power."

**antiphon**

11  I will remember the works of God,
    and call to mind your wonders of old time.
12    I will meditate on all your acts
    and ponder your mighty deeds.
13  Your way, O God, is holy;
    who is so great a god as our God?
14  You are the God who works wonders
    and have declared your power among the peoples.
15  By your strength you have redeemed your people,
    the children of Jacob and Joseph.
16  The waters saw you, O God;
    the waters saw you and trembled;
    the very depths were shaken.
17  The clouds poured out water;
    the skies thundered;
    your arrows flashed to and fro;

18     Your crashing thunder was in the whirlwind,
         your lightning lit up the world,
         the earth trembled and shook.

19   Your way was in the sea,
         and your paths in the great waters,
         yet your footsteps were not seen.

20   You led your people like a flock
         by the hand of Moses and Aaron.

**antiphon**

*Around verse 11, Asaph shifts tone from a personal lamentation to poetic depiction of the crossing of the Sea of Reeds. Surprisingly, the lectionary pairs this text with the passing of the mantle from Elijah to Elisha (2 Kings 2) rather than with the exodus, although Elisha then uses the mantle to part the Jordan River, so a correlation is there. Verse 11, in which the psalmist promises to remember what God has done in the past, nicely echoes the continuity of one generation following another while setting up the second half of the psalm.*

## 78   A Maskil of Asaph.

1    Hear my teaching, O my people;
        incline your ears to the words of my mouth.

2    I will open my mouth in a parable;
        I will declare the mysteries of ancient times.

3    That which we have heard and known,
        and what our ancestors have told us.

4    We will not hide from their children,
        We will recount to generations to come
        the praiseworthy deeds and the power of God,
        and the wonderful works God has done.

5    God gave decrees to Jacob
        and established a law for Israel,
        which commanded them
        to teach their children;

| 6 | That the generations to come might know, |
| | and the children yet unborn, |
| | that they in their turn might tell it to their children, |
| 7 | so that they might put their trust in God |
| | and not forget the deeds of God |
| | but keep the commandments |
| 8 | and not be like their ancestors, |
| | a stubborn and rebellious generation, |
| | a generation whose heart was not steadfast, |
| | whose spirit was not faithful to God. |

**antiphon**

| 9 | The people of Ephraim, armed with the bow, |
| | turned back in the day of battle; |
| 10 | They did not keep the covenant of God |
| | and refused to walk in the law. |
| 11 | They forgot what God had done, |
| | and the wonders shown to them. |
| 12 | God worked marvels in the sight of their ancestors, |
| | in the land of Egypt, in the field of Zoan. |
| 13 | God split open the sea and let them pass through; |
| | and made the waters stand up like walls. |
| 14 | God led them with a cloud by day, |
| | and all the night through with a glow of fire. |
| 15 | God split the hard rocks in the wilderness |
| | and gave them drink as from the great deep. |
| 16 | God brought streams out of the cliff, |
| | and the waters gushed out like rivers. |

**antiphon**

| 17 | But they went on sinning, |
| | rebelling in the desert against the Most High. |
| 18 | They tested God in their hearts, |
| | demanding food for their craving. |
| 19 | They railed against God and said, |
| | "Can God set a table in the wilderness? |
| 20 | True, God struck the rock and waters gushed out, |
| | gullies overflowed; |
| | but is God able to give bread? |
| | Can God provide meat for the people?" |

21 God heard this and was full of wrath;
    a fire was kindled against Jacob,
    and God's anger mounted against Israel;
22     For they had no faith,
    nor did they put their trust in God's saving power.
23 So God commanded the clouds above
    and opened the doors of heaven
24     to rain manna down upon them to eat
    and give them grain from heaven.

antiphon

25 So mortals ate the bread of angels;
    God provided for them food enough.
26 God caused the east wind to blow in the heavens
    and led out the south wind by his might.
27 God rained down flesh upon them like dust,
    winged birds like the sand of the sea,
28     and let it fall in the midst of their camp
    round about their dwellings.
29 So they ate and were well filled,
    for they were given what they craved.
30 But they did not stop their craving,
    though the food was still in their mouths,
31     so God's anger mounted against them.
    God slew their strongest men
    and laid low the youth of Israel.

antiphon

32 In spite of all this, they went on sinning
    and had no faith in God's wonderful works.
33 So God brought their days to an end like a breath
    and their years in sudden terror.
34 Whenever God slew them, they would seek him,
    repent, and diligently search for God.
35 They would remember that God was their rock,
    and the Most High God their redeemer.
36 But they flattered with their mouths
    and lied with their tongues.

37 Their heart was not steadfast,
  and they were not faithful to the covenant.
38 But God was so merciful that their sins were forgiven
  and God did not destroy them;
  many times God held back anger
  and did not permit wrath to be roused,
39   for God remembered that they were but flesh,
  a breath that goes forth and does not return.

**antiphon**

40 How often the people disobeyed in the wilderness
  and offended God in the desert!
41 Again and again they tempted God
  and provoked the Holy One of Israel.
42 They did not remember God's power
  in the day when they were ransomed from the enemy;
43   How God wrought signs in Egypt
  and omens in the field of Zoan.

**antiphon**

44 God turned their rivers into blood,
  so that they could not drink of their streams.
45 God sent swarms of flies among them, which ate them up,
  and frogs, which destroyed them.
46 God gave their crops to the caterpillar,
  the fruit of their toil to the locust.
47 God killed their vines with hail
  and their sycamores with frost.
48 God delivered their cattle to hailstones
  and their livestock to hot thunderbolts.
49 God poured out blazing anger upon them:
  fury, indignation, and distress,
  a troop of destroying angels.
50 God gave full rein to anger;
  and did not spare them from death,
  but delivered them to the plague.
51 God struck down all the firstborn of Egypt,
  the flower of humanity in the dwellings of Ham.

antiphon

52  God led out his people like sheep
        and guided them in the wilderness like a flock.
53  God led them to safety, and they were not afraid;
        but the sea overwhelmed their enemies.
54  God brought them to the holy land,
        the mountain God's right hand had won.
55  God drove out the Canaanites before them,
        apportioned an inheritance to them by lot,
        and made the tribes of Israel dwell in their tents.

antiphon

56  But they tested the Most High God, and were defiant;
        they did not keep the commandments.
57  They turned away and were disloyal like their ancestors;
        they were undependable like a warped bow.
58  They grieved God with their hill-altars
        they provoked displeasure with their idols.

antiphon

59  When God heard this, God was angry
        and utterly rejected Israel.
60  God forsook the shrine at Shiloh,
        the tabernacle where God had lived among the people.
61  God delivered the ark into captivity,
        and glory into the adversary's hand.
62  God gave the people to the sword
        and was angered against God's inheritance.
63  The fire consumed their young men;
        there were no wedding songs for their maidens.
64  Their priests fell by the sword,
        and their widows made no lamentation.

antiphon

65  Then God woke as though from sleep,
        like a warrior refreshed with wine.

66   God struck the enemies on the backside
         and put them to perpetual shame.
67   God rejected the tent of Joseph
         and did not choose the tribe of Ephraim;
68   God chose instead the tribe of Judah
         and Mount Zion, the beloved.
69   God built the sanctuary like the heights of heaven,
         like the earth, founded forever.
70   God chose David as a servant,
         and took him away from the sheepfolds.
71   God brought him from following the ewes,
         to be a shepherd over Jacob, Israel, God's people.
72   So God shepherded them with a faithful and true heart
         and guided them with the skillful hands.

**antiphon**

Asaph covers most of the Torah here: the ten plagues, the exodus, the forty years in the desert, the calling of David, and the destruction of the Temple at Shiloh (which is an obscure story—don't worry if you don't know it). The word "my teaching" in the first verse is actually תּוֹרָתִי —torati, literally "my Torah."

The antiphon is pretty dark because, although the psalm remembers the ancestors, it doesn't have a very high opinion of the ancestors. If you want something a bit brighter, use the antiphon from Psalm 48 instead.

## 79   A Psalm of Asaph

1   O God, the heathen have come into your inheritance;
         they have profaned your holy temple;
         they have made Jerusalem a heap of rubble.
2   They have given the bodies of your servants
         as food for the birds of the air,
         and the flesh of your faithful ones to wild beasts.

157

3   They have shed their blood like water around Jerusalem,
        there was no one to bury them.
4   We have become a reproach to our neighbors,
        an object of scorn and derision to those around us.

**antiphon**

5   How long will you be angry, O God?
        will your fury blaze like fire forever?
6   Pour out your wrath upon the heathen who do not know you
        and upon the kingdoms that have not called upon your Name.
7       For they have devoured Jacob
        and made his dwelling a ruin.
8   Remember not our past sins;
        let your compassion be swift to meet us;
        for we have been brought very low.

**antiphon**

9   Help us, O God our Savior,
        for the glory of your Name.
    Deliver us and forgive us our sins,
        for your Name's sake.
10  Why should the heathen say, "Where is their God?"
    Let it be known among the nations and in our sight
        that you avenge the shedding of your servants' blood.
11  Let the sorrowful sighing of the prisoners come before you,
        and by your great might
        spare those who are condemned to die.
12  May the abuse which they flung at you, O God,
        return seven-fold into their bosoms.
13  For we are your people
        and the sheep of your pasture;
        we will give you thanks forever
        and show forth your praise from age to age.

**antiphon**

  *"How long?" is an interesting question. In the psalms, it's a question usually asked of God by the psalmists in the midst of their distress—check out Psalms 6, 13, 35, 62, 74, 80, 89, 90, 94, and 119. In the Bible as a whole, however, it's just as likely to be God who is putting the question to us, wondering how long it will be necessary to put up with our*

antics. See Exodus 10, Exodus 16, Numbers 14, Proverbs 1, Jeremiah 4, 13, 23, and 31, Hosea 8, and many others. It's healthy to remember that God can be just as exasperated with us as we can be with God.

## 80   To the leader: on Lilies, a Covenant. Of Asaph. A Psalm.

Re - store us, God! Let your face shine that we may be saved.

1    Hear, O Shepherd of Israel,
        leading Joseph like a flock;
    Shine forth, you that are enthroned upon the cherubim.
2        in the presence of Ephraim, Benjamin, and Manasseh.
    Stir up your strength and come to help us.
3    Restore us, O God of hosts;
        show the light of your countenance, and we shall be saved.

**antiphon**

4    O Most High God,
        how long will you be angered
        despite the prayers of your people?
5    You have fed them with the bread of tears;
        you have given them bowls of tears to drink.
6    You have made us the derision of our neighbors,
        and our enemies laugh us to scorn.
7    Restore us, O God of hosts;
        shine your presence and we shall be saved.

**antiphon**

8    You have brought a vine out of Egypt;
        you cast out the nations and planted it.
9    You prepared the ground for it;
        it took root and filled the land.
10   The mountains were covered by its shadow
        and the towering cedar trees by its boughs.
11   You stretched out its tendrils to the Sea
        and its branches to the River.

12  Why have you broken down its wall,
      so that all who pass by pluck off its grapes?
13      The wild boar of the forest has ravaged it,
      and the beasts of the field have grazed upon it.

**antiphon**

14  Turn now, O God of hosts,
      look down from heaven;
      behold and tend this vine;
15      preserve what your right hand has planted.
16  They burn it with fire like rubbish;
      at the rebuke of your countenance let them perish.
17  Let your hand be upon the one at your side,
      and child of humanity you have made strong for yourself.
18  And so will we never turn away from you;
      give us life, that we may call upon your Name.
19  Restore us, O God of hosts;
      shine your presence and we shall be saved.

**antiphon**

*Psalm 78 was pretty down on the Northern Kingdom, claiming that God had cast Israel aside in favor of Judah. Psalm 80 is much more sympathetic, giving voice to the despair the Israelites felt when the Northern Kingdom fell to Assyria. The antiphon here is clear—verses 3, 7, and 19.*

## 81    To the leader: according to The Gittith. Of Asaph.

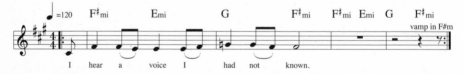

I hear a voice I had not known.

1  Sing with joy to God, our strength,
      and raise a loud shout to the God of Jacob.
2  Raise a song
      and sound the timbrel,
      the merry harp, and the lyre.
3  Blow the ram's-horn at the new moon,
      and at the full moon, the day of our feast.

4   For this is a statute for Israel,
        a law of the God of Jacob,
5       who laid it as a solemn charge upon Joseph,
        when he came out of the land of Egypt.
        I heard an unfamiliar voice.

**antiphon**

6   I eased your shoulder from the burden;
        your hands were set free from bearing the load.
7   You called on me in trouble, and I saved you;
        I answered you from the secret place of thunder
        and tested you at the waters of Meribah.
8   Hear, O my people, and I will admonish you:
        O Israel, if you would but listen to me!
9   There shall be no strange god among you;
        you shall not worship a foreign god.
10  I am God, your God,
        who brought you out of the land of Egypt and said,
        "Open your mouth wide, and I will fill it."

**antiphon**

11  And yet my people did not hear my voice,
        Israel would not obey me.
12  So I gave them over to the stubbornness of their hearts,
        to follow their own devices.
13  Oh, that my people would listen to me!
        that Israel would walk in my ways!
14  I should soon subdue their enemies
        and turn my hand against their foes.
15  Those who hate God would cringe before him,
        and their punishment would last forever.
16  But Israel I would feed with the finest wheat
        and satisfy them with honey from the rock.

**antiphon**

*At the end of verse 5, Asaph hears a voice and from that point on the rest of the psalm relays what was heard. It's very interesting to me that in the introduction the psalmist is clearly familiar with the laws and history of the Israelites, and the message relayed in the* second part of the psalm presumes the same knowledge, yet the voice is still "an unfamiliar voice." No matter how much we think we know about religion and history, God can still surprise us! Also, the word "hear" (אֶשְׁמַע) is in the present/future tense, although most English translations put it in the past. The psalmist is hearing this voice while writing the psalm and, hopefully, we are hearing it today as we sing it.

Incidentally, this antiphon sounds great with guitar power chords and a little distortion.

## 82   A Psalm of Asaph.

You are gods, all of you, chil - dren of the Most High.

1   God takes a stand in the council of heaven;
      and gives judgment in the midst of the gods:
2   "How long will you judge unjustly,
      and show favor to the wicked?
3   Save the weak and the orphan;
      defend the humble and needy;
4      Rescue the weak and the poor;
      deliver them from the power of the wicked.

**antiphon**

5   They do not know, neither do they understand;
      they go about in darkness;
      all the foundations of the earth are shaken.
6   Now I say to you, 'You are gods,
      and all of you children of the Most High;
7      Nevertheless, you shall die like mortals,
      and fall like any prince.'"

**antiphon**

8   Arise, O God, and rule the earth,
      for you shall take all nations for your own.

**antiphon**

*This curious bit of text is unique in the way it presumes a polytheistic world, although both 1 Kings 22 and Job 1 make reference to a "court" in heaven. The text is confusing because* אֱלֹהִים *(elohim), a word for God, is plural, and in this psalm it is translated both as "God" and as "gods." Some suggest that the concept of a heavenly court is borrowed from Canaanite religion, and this psalm is demonstrating the superiority of the Hebrew God. Jewish mystical tradition suggests that the gods referred to are actually the people of Israel, an interpretation that Jesus seems to share when he uses this psalm to fast-talk his way out of getting stoned in John 10.*

## 83    A Song. A Psalm of Asaph.

1    O God, do not be silent;
         do not keep still
         nor hold your peace, O God;

2    For your enemies are in tumult,
         and those who hate you have lifted up their heads.

3    They take secret counsel against your people
         and plot against those whom you protect.

4    They say, "Let us wipe them out from among the nations;
         let the name of Israel be remembered no more."

5    They have conspired together;
         they have made an alliance against you:

6         the clans of Edom and the Ishmaelites;
         the Moabites and the Hagarenes;

7         Gebal, and Ammon, and Amalek;
         the Philistines and those who dwell in Tyre.

8         The Assyrians also have joined them,
         and have come to help the people of Lot.

**antiphon**

9    Do to them as you did to Midian,
         to Sisera, and to Jabin
         at the river of Kishon:

10 They were destroyed at Endor;
    they became like dung upon the ground.
11 Make their leaders like Oreb and Zeëb,
    and all their commanders like Zebah and Zalmunna,
12   who said, "Let us take for ourselves
    the fields of God as our possession."

**antiphon**

13 O my God, make them like whirling dust
    and like chaff before the wind;
14 As fires burn a forest,
    and flames scorch the hills,
15   drive them with your tempest,
    terrify them with your storm;
16 Cover their faces with shame, O God,
    that they may seek your Name.
17 Let them be disgraced and terrified forever;
    let them be put to confusion and perish.
18 Let them know that you,
    whose Name is YHWH,
    alone are supreme over all the earth.

**antiphon**

    *Asaph's last contribution to the Psalter is another prayer for the destruction of Israel's (and, presumably, God's) enemies. Like others of its type, this one never makes it into the lectionary. Although I don't personally condone praying for the destruction of one's enemies, I can completely understand the anger and frustration that come with the feeling that God is silent when God ought to be doing something.*

    *The first verse of this psalm has some wonderful wordplay between* אֵל *(el) and* אַל *(al), both of which are spelled the same in Hebrew (which had no written vowels at the time the Bible was written). El means "God" and al is a verb negation (can be translated as "do not"). By starting every line with one of these words, the psalmist subtly draws a parallel between God and inaction. The final result is like this:*

        Elohim al-domi-lakh         אֱלֹהִים אַל-דֳּמִי-לָךְ
        Al-tekherash               אַל-תֶּחֱרַשׁ
        v'Al-tishkot El.            וְאַל-תִּשְׁקֹט אֵל

    *Although this might not be the most politically correct or the most theologically tidy prayer, it's a very honest one.*

## 84 To the leader: according to The Gittish. Of the Korahites. A Psalm.

How love- ly is your dwell- ing place, my God!

1   How dear to me is your dwelling,
        O God of hosts!
2   I long, I yearn for the courts of God;
        my heart and my flesh rejoice in the living God.
3   The sparrow has found her a house
            and the swallow a nest
            where she may lay her young;
        by the side of your altars, O God of hosts,
            my ruler and my God.
4   Happy are they who dwell in your house!
        they will always be praising you.

**antiphon**

5   Happy are the people whose strength is in you!
        whose hearts are set on the pilgrims' way.
6   Those who go through the valley of Baca
            will find it a place of springs,
        for the early rains have covered it with pools of water.
7   They will climb from height to height,
        and the God of gods will be revealed in Zion.
8   Most High God of hosts,
            hear my prayer;
            hearken, O God of Jacob.
9   Behold our defender, O God;
        and look upon the face of your anointed.

**antiphon**

10  For one day in your courts is better than
            a thousand in my own room,
        and to stand at the threshold of the house of my God
        than to dwell in the tents of the wicked.

11 For the Most High God is both sun and shield;
    God will give grace and glory;
    No good thing will be withheld from those who walk with integrity.
12 O God of hosts,
    happy are they who put their trust in you!

**antiphon**

   When I first saw this psalm, I got excited because I thought it was the source for Mah Tovu, a Jewish hymn sung upon entering a synagogue that begins "How lovely are your tents." Well, after a bit of research I discovered that the Mah Tovu is actually a Frankenstein lyric assembled out of Numbers 24:5 and Psalms 5, 25, 69, and 95. Still, the psalmist here is really excited about entering the Temple, the dwelling place of God.
   It got me thinking, though, about the time David wanted to build a temple for God; God said, "I haven't lived in a house since I brought you out of Egypt. A tent suits me just fine" (2 Samuel 7). Later, the Gospel of John tells us that the word became flesh and pitched its tent among us. Matthew 25 tells us every time we take care of the poor, the hungry, and the naked, we are taking care of Jesus, and the letters of Paul are pretty clear that the Spirit dwells within us. In short, it's good to have songs and liturgies for entering temples and cathedrals, but when we see God in ourselves and in each other, we're gazing at something just as lovely.

## 85   To the leader. Of the Korahites. A Psalm.

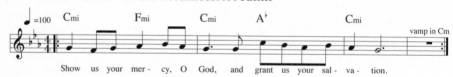

Show us your mer-cy, O God, and grant us your sal-va-tion.

1  You have been gracious to your land, O God,
       you have restored the good fortune of Jacob.
2      You have forgiven the iniquity of your people
       and blotted out their sin.
3      You have withdrawn all your fury
       and turned away from your rage.
4  Restore us then, O God our savior;
       let your anger depart from us.
5  Will you be displeased with us forever?
       Will you prolong your anger from age to age?
6  Will you not give us life again,
       that your people may rejoice in you?

7   Show us your mercy, O God,
        and grant us your salvation.

**antiphon**

8   I will listen to what the Most High God is saying,
        for God is speaking peace to the faithful people
        and to those who turn their hearts to God.
9   Truly, salvation is very near to those who fear,
        that glory may dwell in our land.
10  Mercy and truth have met;
        righteousness and peace kiss each other.
11  Truth springs up from the earth,
        justice looks down from heaven.
12  God will indeed grant prosperity,
        our land will yield its increase.
13  Justice goes before God,
        and peace is a road for God's feet.

**antiphon**

*I used verse 7 for the antiphon because it was the verse that best summarized the entire psalm, a communal cry to God for blessing and deliverance. I almost used verses 10–11, though, because I think they're beautiful. We're all familiar with terms like "righteous indignation" and "holy war," but this psalmist has a vision of righteousness and peace being lovers.*

## 86   A Prayer of David.

1   Bow down your ear, O God,
        answer me,
        for I am poor and in misery.
2   Keep watch over my life, for I am faithful;
        save your servant who trusts in you.
3   Be merciful to me, O God, for you are my God;
        I call upon you all the day long.

4    Gladden the life of your servant,
      for on you, O God, I set my hope.
5    For you, O God, are good and forgiving,
      and great is your love toward all who call upon you.
6    Give ear, O God, to my prayer,
      heed my plea for mercy.
7    In the time of my trouble I call upon you,
      for you will answer me.

**antiphon**

8    Among the gods there is none like you, O God,
      nor anything like your works.
9    All the nations you have made
      will come and worship you, O God,
      and glorify your Name.
10   For you are great and do wondrous things;
      You alone are God.
11   Teach me your way, O God,
      I will walk in your truth;
      knit my heart to you that I may fear your Name.
12   I will thank you, O God, my God, with all my heart,
      and glorify your Name for evermore.
13   For great is your love toward me;
      you have delivered me from the nethermost Pit.

**antiphon**

14   The arrogant rise up against me, O God,
      a violent band seeks my life;
      they have not set you before their eyes.
15   But you, O God,
      are gracious and full of compassion,
      slow to anger, and full of kindness and truth.
16   Turn to me and have mercy upon me;
      give your strength to your servant;
      and save the child of your handmaid.
17   Show me a sign of your favor,
      so that those who hate me may see it and be ashamed;
      because you, O God, have helped me and comforted me.

**antiphon**

*It isn't clear to me whether the psalmist is a mother praying for strength for her son or whether the psalmist is a son who refers to his mother as "God's handmaid," but either way I find it interesting.*

## 87    Of the Korahites. A Psalm. A Song.

1    On the holy mountain stands the city God has founded;
2        God loves the gates of Zion
        more than all the dwellings of Jacob.
3    Glorious things are spoken of you,
        O city of God.
4    I count Rahab and Babylon among those who know me;
        Philistia, Tyre, and Cush—in Zion were they born.
5    Of Zion it shall be said,
        "Everyone was born in her.
    The Most High shall sustain her."
6    God will record, registering the peoples,
        "These also were born there."
7    The singers and the dancers will say,
        "All my fresh springs are in you."

**antiphon**

*Klaus Seybold (Introducing the Psalms, 78) suggests that this rather nonsensical psalm has been jumbled up by scribal errors and can be made clearer by reading it in the following order (note that Seybold follows the Septuagint for this version):*

*2    God loves the gates of Zion*
        *more than all the dwellings of Jacob*
*1    Its foundation stands on the holy mountain,*
*5b    God, the Most High, has established it.*

4a   *I count Rahab and Babel among those who know me,*
       *also Philistia and Tyre, together with Cush;*

5a   *But to Zion I say "Mother",*
       *and "a man is born in her!"*


3   *Glorious things are said of you, O City of God!*

7      *Singers and dancers, all serenade you.*

6   *God, it will be told among the peoples:*
       *"This one was born of Zion!"*

    *In this order, the psalm is a Zionist hymn, expressing Zion's superiority over the Canaanite lands as well as the Northern Kingdom. I wrote the psalm around this interpretation and encourage you to try using the rearranged psalm if you use it in worship.*

## 88   A Song. A Psalm of the Korahites. For the leader: according to Mahalth Leannoth. A Maskil of Heman the Ezrahite.

1   O God, my God, my Savior,
      by day and night I cry to you.

2      Let my prayer reach you;
      incline your ear to my cry.

3   For I am full of trouble;
      my life is at the brink of the grave.

4   I am counted among those who go down to the Pit;
      I am helpless;

5      lost among the dead,
      like the slain who lie in the grave,
      whom you remember no more,
      for they are cut off from your hand.

6   You have laid me in the depths of the Pit,
      in dark places, and in the abyss.

**antiphon**

7   Your anger weighs upon me heavily,
      and all your great waves overwhelm me.

8    You have put my friends far from me;
        you have made me to be abhorred by them;
        I am in prison and cannot get free.

9    My sight has failed me because of trouble;
        God, I have called upon you daily;
        I have stretched out my hands to you.

**antiphon**

10   Do you work wonders for the dead?
        will those who have died stand up and give you thanks?

11   Will your loving-kindness be declared in the grave?
        your faithfulness in the land of destruction?

12   Will your wonders be known in the dark?
        or your righteousness in the land of oblivion?

**antiphon**

13   But as for me, O God, I cry to you for help;
        in the morning my prayer comes before you.

14   God, why have you rejected me?
        why have you hidden your face from me?

15   Ever since my youth, I have been wretched
        and at the point of death;
        I have borne your terrors with a troubled mind.

16   Your blazing anger has swept over me;
        your terrors have destroyed me;

17   They surround me all day long like a flood;
        they encompass me on every side.

18   My friend and my neighbor you have put away from me,
        and darkness is my only companion.

**antiphon**

*Unlike most laments, this one ends after the complaint, never reaching a happy ending. It isn't clear who Heman is; several minor figures in the Bible are named Heman, but none of them are called an Ezrahite. My theory is that this was written while the psalmist was defending Castle Greyskull and the antiphon reflects this.*

## 89  A Maskil of Ethan the Ezrahite.

Bless - ed  is  God  for - ev - er,  A - men  and  A - men!

1   Your love, O God, forever will I sing;
      from age to age my mouth will proclaim your faithfulness.
2   For I am persuaded that your love is established forever;
      you have set your faithfulness firmly in the heavens.

**antiphon**

3   "I have made a covenant with my chosen one;
      I have sworn an oath to David, my servant:
4      'I will establish your line forever,
      and preserve your throne for all generations.'"

**antiphon**

5   The heavens bear witness to your wonders, O God,
      and to your faithfulness in the assembly of the holy ones;
6   For who in the skies can be compared to God?
      who is like God among the gods?
7      God is much to be feared in the council of the holy ones,
      great and terrible to all those round about him.
8   O Most High God of hosts,
      who is mighty like you?

**antiphon**

    O mighty God, your faithfulness is all around you.
9      You rule the raging of the sea
      and still the surging of its waves.
10  You have crushed Rahab of the deep with a deadly wound;
      you have scattered your enemies with your mighty arm.
11  Yours are the heavens,
      the earth, too,
      the foundations of the world
      and all that is in it.

12  North and South—
       You created them.
       Tabor and Hermon rejoice in your Name.
13  You have a mighty arm;
       strong is your hand
       and high is your right hand.
14  Righteousness and justice are the foundations of your throne;
       love and truth go before You.

**antiphon**

15  Happy are the people who know the festal shout!
       they walk, O God, in the light of your presence.
16  They rejoice daily in your Name;
       they are jubilant in your righteousness.
17  For you are the glory of their strength,
       and by your favor our might is exalted.
18  Truly, God is our ruler;
       The Holy One of Israel is our sovereign.

**antiphon**

19  You spoke once in vision and said to your faithful people:
       "I have set the crown upon a warrior
       and have exalted one chosen out of the people.
20  I have found David, my servant;
       with my holy oil have I anointed him.
21  My hand will hold him fast
       and my arm will make him strong.
22  No enemy shall deceive him,
       nor any wicked man bring him down.
23  I will crush his foes before him
       and strike down those who hate him.
24  My faithfulness and love shall be with him,
       and he shall be victorious through my Name.
25  I shall make his dominion extend
       from the Great Sea to the River.
26  He will say to me,
       'You are my Protector, my God, and the rock of my salvation.'

**antiphon**

27  I will make him my firstborn
        and higher than the rulers of the earth.
28  I will keep my love for him forever,
        and my covenant will stand firm for him.
29  I will establish his line forever
        and his throne as the days of heaven."
30  "If his children forsake my law
        and do not walk according to my judgments;
31      If they break my statutes
        and do not keep my commandments;
32      I will punish their transgressions with a rod
        and their iniquities with the lash;

**antiphon**

33  But I will not take my love from him,
        nor let my faithfulness prove false.
34  I will not break my covenant,
        nor change what has gone out of my lips.
35  Once for all I have sworn by my holiness:
        'I will not lie to David.
36  His line shall endure forever
        and his throne as the sun before me;
37      It shall stand fast for evermore like the moon,
        the abiding witness in the sky.'"

**antiphon**

38  But you have cast off and rejected your anointed;
        you have become enraged.
39  You have broken your covenant with your servant,
        defiled his crown, and hurled it to the ground.
40  You have breached all the walls
        and laid strongholds in ruins.
41  All who pass by despoil him;
        he has become the scorn of his neighbors.
42  You have exalted the right hand of his foes
        and made all his enemies rejoice.
43  You have turned back the edge of his sword
        and have not sustained him in battle.

44 You have put an end to his splendor
    and cast his throne to the ground.
45 You have cut short the days of his youth
    and have covered him with shame.

**antiphon**

46 How long will you hide yourself, O God?
    How long will your anger burn like fire?
47 Remember, God, how short life is,
    how frail you have made all flesh.
48 Who can live and not see death?
    who can be saved from the power of the grave?
49 Where, God, is your loving-kindnesses of old,
    which you promised David in your faithfulness?
50 Remember, God, how your servant is mocked,
    how I carry in my bosom the taunts of many peoples,
51     the taunts your enemies have hurled, O God,
    which they hurl at the heels of your anointed.

**antiphon**

52 Blessed be God for evermore!
    Amen and Amen.

**antiphon**

This Royal Lament ends Book III of the Psalter. The text spans quite a bit of history: verses 5–15 are a fragment of an old hymn, verses 19–37 are a restatement of God's covenant with David in 2 Samuel 7, and verses 38–51 contrast a difficult exilic or postexilic experience with the "glory days" of David's monarchy. Of course, since this psalm is read in Advent, many will also interpret it to be a comparison between David's life and Jesus' life. Finally, adding our own experience to the psalm leaves us with a LOT of layers. Rather than attempt to summarize all of this in a single verse, I used the benediction that closes Book III; the Hebrew לְעוֹלָם ("to eternity") communicates that humanity's relationship with God stretches across time and generations. Since similar benedictions close out Books I, II, and IV, this antiphon could also be used for Psalms 41, 72, or 106.

# Book IV

## 90    A Prayer of Moses, the man of God.

From age to age, you are God. From age to age, you are God.

1    God, you have been our refuge in every generation.
2    Before the mountains were brought forth,
        or the land and the earth were born,
        from age to age you are God.
3    You turn us back to the dust and say,
        "Go back, O child of earth."
4    For a thousand years in your sight
        are like yesterday when it is past
        and like a watch in the night.
5    You sweep us away like a dream;
        we fade away suddenly like the grass.
6        In the morning it is green and flourishes;
        in the evening it is dried up and withered.

**antiphon**

7    For we consume away in your displeasure;
        we are afraid because of your wrathful indignation.
8    Our iniquities you have set before you,
        and our secret sins in the light of your countenance.
9    When you are angry, all our days are gone;
        we bring our years to an end like a sigh.
10   The span of our life is seventy years,
        perhaps in strength even eighty;
        yet the sum of them is but labor and sorrow.
     They pass away quickly and we are gone.

11  Who regards the power of your wrath?
Who rightly fears your indignation?
12  So teach us to number our days
that we may apply our hearts to wisdom.

**antiphon**

13  Return, O God;
How long will you tarry?
Be gracious to your servants.
14  Satisfy us by your loving-kindness in the morning;
so shall we rejoice and be glad all the days of our life.
15  Make us glad by the measure of the days that you afflicted us
and the years in which we suffered adversity.
16  Show your servants your works
and your splendor to their children.
17  May the graciousness of God our God be upon us;
prosper the work of our hands;
prosper our handiwork.

**antiphon**

*Book IV opens with the only psalm attributed to Moses, and it's easy to imagine him praying such a prayer while preparing to die just before the Israelites entered the promised land (Deuteronomy 34). At the age of 120, Moses was not exactly a young man, but he might have felt that he was passing away prematurely, before his work was done. In this interpretation, verse 3 ("turn back you mortals") could refer to the first time that the Israelites almost crossed into Canaan but were turned back by God (Numbers 13–14) and the end of the psalm could be Moses praying for his people's future, a future he will never see. In this way, Psalm 90 is similar to John 17, when Jesus prays for his disciples in preparation for his death.*

## 91

1  They who dwell in the shelter of the Most High,
abide under the shadow of the Almighty.

2       They shall say to God,
          "You are my refuge and my stronghold,
          my God in whom I put my trust."

3       God shall deliver you from the snare of the hunter
          and from the deadly pestilence.

4    God shall cover you with pinions,
          and you shall find refuge under God's wings;
          God's faithfulness shall be a shield and buckler.

5    You shall not be afraid of any terror by night,
          nor of the arrow that flies by day;

6       Of the plague that stalks in the darkness,
          nor of the sickness that lays waste at mid-day.

7    A thousand shall fall at your side
          and ten thousand at your right hand,
          but it shall not come near you.

**antiphon**

8    Your eyes have only to behold
          to see the reward of the wicked.

9    Because you have made God your refuge,
          and the Most High your habitation,

10      There shall no evil happen to you,
          neither shall any plague come near your dwelling.

11   For God shall give his angels charge over you,
          to keep you in all your ways.

12   They shall bear you in their hands,
          lest you dash your foot against a stone.

13   You shall tread upon the lion and the adder;
          you shall trample the lions and serpents.

**antiphon**

14   Because they are bound to me in love, I will deliver them;
          I will protect them, because they know my Name.

15   They shall call upon me, and I will answer them;
          I am with them in trouble;
          I will rescue them and bring them to honor.

16      With long life will I satisfy them
          and show them my salvation.

**antiphon**

*Although this psalm is used every day in compline, I found it hard to get away from the Lenten overtones. The temptations of Christ in the desert not only make for a powerful story, they also demonstrate how Scripture can mean astonishingly different things depending on who is quoting it. It didn't mean to Jesus what it meant to the devil, it didn't necessarily mean to Matthew and Luke what it meant to the psalmist, and it probably doesn't mean to me what it means to you.*

## 92   A Psalm. A Song for the Sabbath Day.

The right-eous flour-ish and grow; in old age they still pro-duce fruit.

1  It is a good thing to give thanks to God,
     and to sing praises to your Name, O Most High;
2  To tell of your loving-kindness early in the morning
     and of your faithfulness in the night season;
3  On the psaltery, and on the lyre,
     and to the melody of the harp.
4  For you have made me glad by your acts, O God;
     I shout for joy because of the works of your hands.
5  God, how great are your works!
     your thoughts are very deep.
6  The dullard does not know,
     nor does the fool understand,
7      that though the wicked grow like weeds,
     and all the workers of iniquity flourish,
     they flourish only to be destroyed forever;

**antiphon**

8  But you, O God, are exalted for evermore.

**antiphon**

9  Surely your enemies, O God,
     surely, your enemies shall perish,
     and the wicked be scattered.
10  But my horn you have exalted like the horns of wild bulls;
     I am anointed with fresh oil.

11   My eyes also gloat over my enemies,
          and hear the doom of the wicked who rise up against me.
12   The righteous shall flourish like a palm tree,
          and shall spread abroad like a cedar of Lebanon.
13        Those who are planted in the house of God
          shall flourish in the courts of our God;
14   They shall still bear fruit in old age;
          they shall be green and succulent;
15        they show how upright God is,
          my rock, in whom there is no fault.

**antiphon**

*The Bible is full of stories of people bringing hope and change into the world in their old age. I once heard John Bell describe the Christmas story as a story for old people because, with the exception of Mary, everyone in the story is elderly! The best worship communities I have ever been part of have been intergenerational, and if we in the emergent church don't have a relationship with our elders, it is our loss.*

## 93

1    God is sovereign,
          robed in grandeur;
          God is robed
          and girded with strength.
     The world stands firm
          it cannot be shaken.
2    Since the world began, your throne has stood;
          You are from everlasting.
3    The oceans have lifted up, O God,
          the oceans have lifted up their voice;
          the oceans have lifted up their pounding waves.
4    Mightier than the sound of many waters,
          mightier than the breakers of the sea,
          mightier is God who dwells on high.

5   Your testimonies are very sure,
        and holiness adorns your house, O God,
        forever and for evermore.

**antiphon**

*The phrase "YWHW is King!" is central here, and this psalm begins a series of "Enthronement Psalms" that include Psalms 95–99 (and some include Psalm 47). Unlike the royal psalms, which depict the king as the chosen servant of God, these psalms declare that it is God and God alone who is king. I was sorely tempted to translate this as "God is commander-in-chief," which is more relevant to our context, more subversive, and gender-neutral, but ultimately decided it was too clunky for singing. Instead I encourage anyone who wants to replace "king" with "queen" to do so!*

*This is also one of the most poetic psalms to read in the original Hebrew. The BCP text doesn't do a very good job of depicting the gracefully succinct nature of this psalm, which includes alliteration, rhyme, assonance, and onomatopoeia:*

| | |
|---|---|
| YHWH malakh | יְהוָה מָלָךְ, |
| Geut lavesh | גֵּאוּת לָבֵשׁ: |
| Lavesh YHWH | לָבֵשׁ יְהוָה, |
| Oz hitazar | עֹז הִתְאַזָּר; |

*I tried to capture the more succinct feel in the antiphon.*

**94**

1   O Most High, God of vengeance,
        O God of vengeance, show yourself.
2   Rise up, O Judge of the world;
        give the arrogant their just deserts.
3   How long shall the wicked, O God,
        how long shall the wicked triumph?
4       They bluster in their insolence;
        all evildoers are full of boasting.

5    They crush your people, O God,
        and afflict your chosen nation.
6        They murder the widow and the stranger
        and put the orphans to death.
7        Yet they say, "God does not see,
        the God of Jacob takes no notice."

**antiphon**

8    Consider well, you dullards among the people;
        when will you fools understand?
9    Does the one who planted the ear, not hear?
        Does the one who formed the eye, not see?
10   Does the one who admonishes the nations, not punish?
        Does the one who teaches all the world have no knowledge?
11   God knows human thoughts are a puff of wind.

**antiphon**

12   Happy are they whom you instruct, O God!
        whom you teach out of your law;
13        to give them rest in evil days,
        until a pit is dug for the wicked.
14   For God will not abandon the people,
        nor forsake God's own.
15   For judgment will again be just,
        and all the true of heart will follow it.

**antiphon**

16   Who rose up for me against the wicked?
     Who took my part against the evildoers?
17   If God had not come to my help,
        I should soon have dwelt in the land of silence.
18   As often as I said, "My foot has slipped,"
        your love, O God, upheld me.
19   When many cares fill my mind,
        your assurance sooths my soul.

**antiphon**

20 Can a corrupt tribunal have any part with you,
    one which frames evil into law?
21 They conspire against the life of the just
    and condemn the innocent to death.
22 But God has become my stronghold,
    and my God, the rock of my trust.
23 God will turn their wickedness back upon them
    and destroy them in their own malice;
    God, our God, will destroy them.

**antiphon**

*This is the only psalm in this section that is not part of the "YWHW is King" series, and it's also the only psalm in this section that was left out of the lectionary. It's not surprising, considering that this is a prayer calling down vengeance on the psalmist's enemies. Any psalm that ends with "God, our God, will destroy them" is bound to be unpopular in today's pluralist world. The Hebrew uses a lot of repetition, often repeating the same word for emphasis, which gives many of the verses a stuttered feel. I tried to reproduce this by writing in three bar phrases that, hopefully, make the antiphon seem lopsided.*

*I also used G to E (a chromatic mediant) for the turnaround—it's a harmonic movement used in a lot of Westerns from the 60s and 70s. This song is about vengeance, and all the best revenge movies are spaghetti westerns. While I was working on it, though, my girlfriend commented that it sounded a bit like Metallica's "The Unforgiven," which uses similar chords. Further, each line of the chorus begins with a near-repetition, just like Psalm 94, so maybe Metallica was looking at this psalm when they wrote it. . . .*

**95**

1 Come, let us sing to God;
    let us shout for joy to the Rock of our salvation.
2 Let us come before God's presence with thanksgiving
    and raise a loud shout with psalms.
3 For God is a great God,
    and a great ruler above all gods.

4    In God's hand are the caverns of the earth,
         and the heights of the hills, as well.
5    The sea is God's, who made it,
         and God's hands molded the dry land.

**antiphon**

6    Come, let us bow down, and bend the knee,
         and kneel before God our Maker.
7    For the Most High is our God,
         and we are the people of God's pasture and the flock of God's hand.
     Oh, that today you would hearken to God's voice!
8        Harden not your hearts,
         as your forebears did in the wilderness,
         at Meribah, and on that day at Massah,
         when they tempted me.
9        tested me, though they had seen my works.
10   Forty years long I detested that generation.
     I thought, "This people are wayward in their hearts;
         they do not know my ways."
11   So I swore in my wrath,
         "They shall not enter into my rest."

**antiphon**

*I first wrote this antiphon as a part of the Disco Episco, a seminary project in which j. Snodgrass and I assembled an entire eucharistic liturgy comprised solely of disco lyrics. (Our dismissal was "Go on now go, walk out the door.") Discerning listeners will notice a reference to Disco Inferno in the bass line. Since then, I've discovered that this psalm is used in the Anglican liturgy of morning prayer. Who doesn't love the sound of disco in the morning?*

**96**

| | | | | | | | | | |
|---|---|---|---|---|---|---|---|---|---|
| A - | scribe | to | God | | the | glor - | y | of The | Name. |

Bring an of - fer - ing and come in - to the courts.

*vamp in Gm*

1   Sing to God a new song;
      sing to God, all the whole earth.
2   Sing to God and bless the Name;
      proclaim the good news of salvation from day to day.
3   Declare God's glory among the nations
      and God's wonders among all peoples.
4   For great is God and greatly to be praised;
      our God is more to be feared than all gods.
5   As for all the gods of the nations, they are but idols;
      but it is our God who made the heavens.
6   Oh, the majesty and magnificence of God's presence!
      Oh, the power and the splendor of God's sanctuary!

**antiphon**

7   Ascribe to God, you families of the peoples;
      ascribe to God honor and power.
8   Ascribe to God the honor due the Name;
      bring offerings and come into God's courts.
9   Worship God in the beauty of holiness;
      let the whole earth tremble before him.
10  Tell it out among the nations: "God is Sovereign!
      God has made the world so firm that it cannot be moved;
      and will judge the peoples with equity."
11  Let the heavens rejoice, and let the earth be glad;
      let the sea thunder and all that is in it;
12      let the field be joyful and all that is therein.
      Then shall all the trees of the wood shout for joy
13      before God, who is coming,
      who is coming to judge the earth.

God will judge the world with righteousness
and the peoples with truth.

**antiphon**

*Much of this psalm has been adapted from other psalms. Verses 7–9 come from Psalm 29:1–3, verse 10 comes from Psalm 93:1–2, and verses 11–13 come from Psalm 98:7–9. The quotations are not verbatim, however. For example, instead of calling upon heavenly beings to worship God, verses 7–9 call upon the nations, placing this psalm in contrast with both Psalm 29, from which the quote was taken, and with Psalm 95, which immediately precedes it.*

*I wrote the antiphon as a two-part canon, mimicking the rise and fall of the seas mentioned in verse 11. The antiphon works just fine in unison, however.*

**97**

1    God reigns!
Let the earth rejoice;
    the many islands be glad.

2    Clouds and darkness surround God,
    righteousness and justice are the foundations of God's throne.

3    A fire goes before God
    and burns up his enemies on every side.

4    Lightning lights up the world;
    the earth sees it and is afraid.

5    The mountains melt like wax at the presence of God,
    at the presence of God of the whole earth.

6    The heavens declare righteousness,
    and all the peoples see glory.

**antiphon**

7 All who worship carved images
  and delight in false gods
  are dismayed.
  Bow down before our God, all you gods.

8 Zion hears and is glad,
  and the cities of Judah rejoice,
  because of your judgments, O God.

9 For you are God, supreme over all the earth;
  you are exalted far above all gods.

**antiphon**

10 God loves those who hate evil.
  God preserves the lives of saints
  and delivers them from the hand of the wicked.

11 Light has sprung up for the righteous,
  and joyful gladness for those who are truehearted.

12 Rejoice in God, you righteous,
  and give thanks to the holy Name.

**antiphon**

*Unlike ancient Israel, we don't see pluralism as a threat to national identity, and we don't worry too much about idol worshipers. We still live in an image-obsessed culture, however, and instead of worshiping graven images we've started worshiping image itself, but youth, wealth, recognition, and beauty can't take the place of God.*

## 98 A Psalm.

Let the sea roar and the moun - tains sing at the pres - ence of the Lord!

1 Sing a new song to God,
  who has done marvelous things.
  whose right hand and holy arm
  have won victory.

2 God has made known victory;
  and displayed righteousness in the sight of the nations.

3 God remembers mercy and faithfulness to the house of Israel,
  all the ends of the earth have seen the victory of our God.

4    Shout with joy, all you lands;
         lift up your voice, rejoice, and sing.
5    Sing to God with the harp,
         with the harp and the voice of song.
6    With trumpets and the sound of the horn
         shout with joy before God, the Most High.
7    Let the sea make a noise and all that is in it,
         the lands and those who dwell therein.
8    Let the rivers clap their hands,
         let the hills ring out with joy
         before God,
9    who comes to judge the earth.
    In righteousness, God shall judge the world
         and the peoples with equity.

**antiphon**

*Some psalms want to restrict the grace of God to Israel. This psalm claims the exact opposite.*

## 99

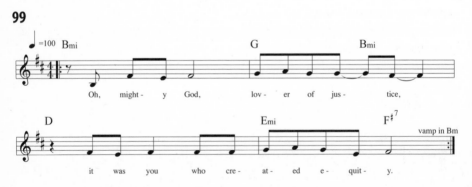

1    God reigns, let the people tremble.
         God is enthroned upon the cherubim, let the earth shake.
2    God is great in Zion
         and is high above all peoples.
3    Let them confess the Name, which is great and awesome;
         God is the Holy One.

**antiphon**

4    "O mighty ruler, lover of justice,
         you have established equity;
         you have executed righteous justice in Jacob."
5    Proclaim the greatness of God, our God
         and fall down before God's footstool;
         God is the Holy One.

**antiphon**

6    Moses and Aaron among the priests,
         Samuel among those who call upon the Name,
         they called upon God,
         who answered them.
7    God spoke to them out of the pillar of cloud;
         and kept the testimonies and the decree that were given to them.
8    "O God, our God, you answered them indeed;
         you were a God who forgave them,
         yet punished them for their evil deeds."

**antiphon**

9    Proclaim the greatness of God, our God,
         and worship him upon the holy hill;
         for God, our God, is the Holy One.

**antiphon**

*Equity didn't exist in the days of Moses and Aaron, nor in the days of Samuel, nor does it exist in our world today. There are still rich and poor, masters and slaves, oppressors and oppressed. Where other psalmists would pray for an end to such things, however, this psalmist boldly declares that they've already ended, seeing the world as it ought to be rather than as it is. I love it.*

## 100　A Psalm of Thanksgiving.

For God is good, and God's mer - cy is ev - er - las - ting.

1　Be joyful in God, all you lands;
2　　serve God with gladness
　　come before God's presence with a song.
3　Know this: God is the Most High,
　　who has made us, and we are God's;
　　we are God's people and the flock of God's pasture.
4　Enter the gates with thanksgiving,
　　the courts with praise;
　Praise God!
　Bless God's Name!
5　For God is good;
　　God's mercy is everlasting;
　　and God's faithfulness endures from age to age.

**antiphon**

*This psalm is a hymn, meant to be used by a gathered community for worship. It alternates invitations to praise with declarations of faith, and works well at the beginning of a service or as a creed.*

## 101　Of David. A Psalm.

I will stu - dy the way of the blame - less.

When will it come to me?

1　I will sing of mercy and justice;
　　to you, O God, will I sing praises.
2　I will strive to follow a blameless course;
　　oh, when will you come to me?
　I will walk with sincerity of heart within my house.

3   I will set no worthless thing before my eyes;
        I hate the doers of evil deeds;
        they shall not remain with me.
4   A crooked heart shall be far from me;
        I will not know evil.
5   Those who in secret slander their neighbors I will destroy;
        I cannot endure the haughty and proud.
6   My eyes are upon the faithful in the land,
        that they may dwell with me.
    Those who lead a blameless life
        shall be my servants.
7   Those who act deceitfully
        shall not dwell in my house.
    Those who tell lies
        shall not continue in my sight.
8   Each morning I will destroy
        all the wicked in the land,
        that I may root out all evildoers
        from the city of God.

**antiphon**

*To me, this psalm reads like someone in power trying to imagine what governing justly would look like. If it weren't for the first two verses, it would seem like a boastful manifesto, but the initial question reveals a level of self-doubt that humanizes the psalmist.*

## 102   A prayer of one afflicted, when faint and pleading before God.

1   God, hear my prayer,
        let my cry come before you.
2   Hide not your face from me
        in the day of my trouble.

Incline your ear to me;
 when I call, make haste to answer me,

3 For my days drift away like smoke,
 and my bones are hot as burning coals.

4 My heart is smitten like grass and withered,
 so that I forget to eat my bread.

5 Because of the voice of my groaning
 I am but skin and bones.

6 I have become like a vulture in the wilderness,
 an owl among the ruins.

7 I lie awake and groan;
 a sparrow, lonely on a house-top.

**antiphon**

8 My enemies revile me all day long,
 my deriders use my name to curse.

9 For I have eaten ashes for bread
 and mingled my drink with weeping.

10 Because of your indignation and wrath
 you have lifted me up and thrown me away.

11 My days pass away like a shadow,
 I wither like the grass.

**antiphon**

12 But you, O God, endure forever,
 and your Name from age to age.

13 You will arise and have compassion on Zion,
 for it is time to have mercy upon her;
 indeed, the appointed time has come.

14 For your servants love her very rubble,
 and are moved to pity even for her dust.

15 The nations shall fear your Name, O God,
 and all the rulers of the earth your glory.

16 For God will build up Zion,
 and glory will appear.

17 God will look with favor on the prayer of the homeless;
 and will not despise their plea.

**antiphon**

18   Let this be written for a future generation,
        so that a people yet unborn may praise God.
19   For God looked down from the holy place on high,
        beheld the earth from the heavens,
20       to hear the groan of the captive
        to set free those condemned to die,
21       that they may declare in Zion the Name of God,
        and praise in Jerusalem;
22       when the peoples are gathered together,
        and the nations also, to serve God.

**antiphon**

23   God has brought down my strength before my time;
        and shortened the number of my days;
24   And I said, "O my God,
        do not take me away in the midst of my days;
        your years endure throughout all generations.
25   In the beginning, O God, you laid the foundations of the earth,
        and the heavens are the work of your hands;
26   They shall perish, but you will endure;
        they all shall wear out like a garment;
        as clothing you will change them and they pass away.
27   But you are always the same, and your years never end.
28       The children of your servants shall continue,
        and their offspring shall stand fast in your sight."

**antiphon**

*For those keeping track, this is the fifth Penitential Psalm, but it seems that the psalmist is more interested in being delivered from a degenerative illness and an early death than in expressing contrition for sins. I find it especially interesting that rather than ending with a declaration of God's healing deliverance, as in other psalms, the psalmist ends by taking comfort in the knowledge that future generations would be established in God's presence. For this writer, the hope of God comes in the creation of something new rather than the preservation of something old.*

*This antiphon works best with a guitar strumming double time.*

## 103  Of David

Like the grass that grows and fades, is the cy - cle of our days.

1  Bless God, O my soul,
    all my being bless the holy Name.
2  Bless God, O my soul,
    and forget not all God's benefits.
3  God forgives all your sins
    and heals all your infirmities;
4  God redeems your life from the grave
    and crowns you with mercy and loving-kindness;
5  God satisfies you with good things,
    and your youth is renewed like an eagle's.

**antiphon**

6  God executes righteousness
    and judgment for all who are oppressed.
7  God made ways known to Moses
    and works to the children of Israel.
8  God is full of compassion and mercy,
    slow to anger, and of great kindness.
9  God will not always accuse us,
    nor stay angry forever.
10  God has not dealt with us according to our sins,
    nor rewarded us according to our wickedness.

**antiphon**

11  As the heavens are high above the earth,
    so is God's mercy great upon those who fear.
12  As far as the east is from the west,
    so far has God removed our sins from us.
13  As a parent cares for children,
    so does God care for those who fear.
14  For God knows of what we are made;
    and remembers that we are but dust.

**antiphon**

15 Our days are like the grass;
　　we flourish like a flower of the field;
16 　when the wind goes over it, it is gone,
　　and its place shall know it no more.
17 But the merciful goodness of God endures forever
　　on those who fear,
　　and God's righteousness is on the children's children;
18 　on those who keep the covenant
　　and remember the commandments and do them.
19 God has set a throne in heaven,
　　and God's sovereignty has dominion over all.

**antiphon**

20 Bless God, you angels,
　　you mighty ones who do God's bidding,
　　and hearken to the voice of the word.
21 Bless God, all the hosts,
　　you ministers who do God's will.
22 　Bless God, all you works,
　　in all places God's dominion;
　　bless God, O my soul.

**antiphon**

　　*This psalm feels like a CliffsNotes version of Ecclesiastes: Humanity is impermanent but God is eternal, and wisdom lies in keeping God's commandments. To echo this theme of generations of humanity passing like grass, I wrote a chord cycle that moves but never resolves.*

## 104

1 Bless God, O my soul;
　　O God, my God, how excellent is your greatness!
　　you are clothed with majesty and splendor.

2      You wrap yourself with light as with a cloak
          and spread out the heavens like a curtain.

3    You lay the beams of your chambers in the waters above;
          you make the clouds your chariot;
          you ride on the wings of the wind.

4    You make the winds your messengers
          and flames of fire your servants.

**antiphon**

5    You have set the earth upon its foundations,
          so that it never shall move at any time.

6    You covered it with the deep as with a mantle;
          the waters stood higher than the mountains.

7    At your rebuke they fled;
          at the voice of your thunder they hastened away.

8    They went up into the hills and down to the valleys beneath,
          to the places you had appointed for them.

9    You set the limits that they should not pass;
          they shall not again cover the earth.

**antiphon**

10   You send the springs into the valleys;
          they flow between the mountains.

11     All the beasts of the field drink from them,
          the wild asses quench their thirst.

12   Beside them the birds of the air make their nests
          and sing among the branches.

13   You water the mountains from your dwelling on high;
          the earth is fully satisfied by the fruit of your works.

**antiphon**

14   You make grass grow for flocks and herds
          and plants to serve humanity
          that they may bring forth food from the earth,

15     and wine to gladden our hearts,
          oil to make a cheerful countenance,
          and bread to strengthen the heart.

16   The trees of God are full of sap,
          the cedars of Lebanon which he planted,

17      in which the birds build their nests,
          and in whose tops the stork makes his dwelling.

18  The high hills are a refuge for the mountain goats,
          and the stony cliffs for the rock badgers.

**antiphon**

19  You appointed the moon to mark the seasons,
          and the sun knows the time of its setting.

20  You make darkness that it may be night,
          in which all the beasts of the forest prowl.

21  The lions roar after their prey
          and seek their food from God.

22  The sun rises, and they slip away
          and lay themselves down in their dens.

23  People go forth to work
          and labor until the evening.

**antiphon**

24  O God, how manifold are your works!
          in wisdom you have made them all;
          the earth is full of your creatures.

25  Yonder is the great and wide sea
          with its living things too many to number,
          creatures both small and great.

26  There move the ships,
          and there is that Leviathan which you made for sport.

27  All of them look to you
          to give them their food in due season.

28  You give it to them; they gather it;
          you open your hand, and they are filled with good things.

29           Hide your face, and they are terrified;
          you take away their breath, and they die
          returning to dust.

30           Send forth your Spirit, and they are created;
          and you renew the face of the earth.

**antiphon**

31  May the glory of God endure forever;
          may God rejoice in all works.

32 God looks at the earth and it trembles;
   God touches the mountains and they smoke.
33 I will sing to God as long as I live;
   I will praise my God while I have my being.
34 May these words of mine be pleasing;
   I will rejoice in God.
35 Let sinners be consumed out of the earth,
   and the wicked be no more.
   Bless God, O my soul.
   Hallelujah!

**antiphon**

The very first Transmission was in October 2006 at a Christian Culture Festival in the UK called Greenbelt. Back then Transmission consisted of just two people, Bowie Snodgrass and me, and we decided to do our first service among our close friends from Moot, an emerging community in London. The ritual focused on fashion, embodiment, and the relationship between inner transformation and outer transformation and culminated in the assembled congregation putting together outfits and throwing an impromptu fashion show. Wild, I know, but strangely moving.

This antiphon was written for that service, the first Transmission.

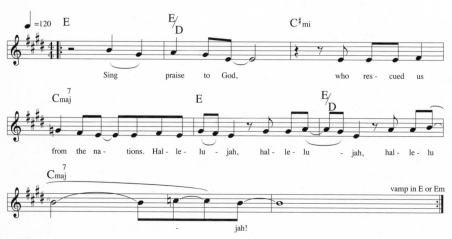

1   Give thanks to God
       call upon the Name;
    make known God's deeds among the peoples.

2   Sing to God, sing praises,
        speak of all the marvelous works.
3   Glory in the holy Name;
        let the hearts of those who seek God rejoice.
4   Search for God and God's strength;
        continually seek God's face.
5   Remember the marvels done,
        the wonders and judgments of God's mouth,
6   O offspring of Abraham, the servant,
        O children of Jacob, the chosen.

**antiphon**

7   God is the Most High,
        whose judgments prevail in all the world.
8   God has always been mindful of the covenant,
        the promise made for a thousand generations:
9   The covenant made with Abraham,
        the oath sworn to Isaac,
10     established as a statute for Jacob,
        an everlasting covenant for Israel,
11     saying, "To you will I give the land of Canaan
        to be your allotted inheritance."

**antiphon**

12  When they were few in number,
        of little account, and sojourners in the land,
13     wandering from nation to nation
        and from one kingdom to another,
14  God let no one oppress them
        and rebuked rulers for their sake,
15     saying, "Do not touch my anointed;
        do my prophets no harm."

**antiphon**

16  Then God called for a famine in the land
        and destroyed the supply of bread.
17  God sent a man before them,
        Joseph, who was sold as a slave.

18 They bruised his feet in fetters;
    his neck they put in an iron collar.
19 Until his prediction came to pass,
    the word of God tested him.
20 The king sent and released him;
    the ruler of the peoples set him free.
21 He set him as a master over his household,
    as a ruler over all his possessions,
22    to instruct his princes according to his will
    and to teach his elders wisdom.
23 Israel came into Egypt,
    and Jacob became a sojourner in the land of Ham.

**antiphon**

24 God made the people exceedingly fruitful;
    and made them stronger than their enemies
25 Whose heart he turned, so that they hated his people,
    and dealt unjustly with his servants.

**antiphon**

26 God sent Moses, the servant,
    and Aaron, the chosen.
27 They worked signs among them,
    and portents in the land of Ham.
28 God sent darkness, and it grew dark;
    but the Egyptians rebelled against God's words.
29 God turned their waters into blood
    and caused their fish to die.
30 Their land was overrun by frogs,
    in the very chambers of their rulers.

**antiphon**

31 God spoke, and there came swarms of insects
    and gnats within all their borders.
32 God gave them hailstones instead of rain,
    and flames of fire throughout their land.
33 God blasted their vines and their fig trees
    and shattered every tree in their country.

34  God spoke, and the locust came,
       and young locusts without number,
35       which ate up all the green plants in their land
       and devoured the fruit of their soil.
36  God struck down the firstborn of their land,
       the first fruits of all their strength.
37  God led out his people with silver and gold;
       in all their tribes there was not one that stumbled.
38  Egypt was glad of their going,
       because they were afraid of them.

**antiphon**

39  God spread out a cloud for a covering
       and a fire to give light in the night season.
40  They asked, and quails appeared,
       God satisfied them with bread from heaven.
41  God opened the rock, and water flowed,
       so the river ran in the dry places.
42  For God remembered the holy word
       and Abraham, the servant.
43  So the people were led forth with gladness,
       the chosen with shouts of joy.
44  God gave the people the lands of the nations,
       and they took the fruit of others' toil,
45       that they might keep the statutes
       and observe the laws.
       Hallelujah!

**antiphon**

   *Although not an official Psalm of Asaph, it seems like 105 ought to be. Not only does it have Asaph's characteristic emphasis on history and narrative, but in 1 Chronicles 16, Asaph sings these exact words at David's command when the Ark is brought into Jerusalem for the first time! The psalmist apparently sees the installation of the Ark as the culmination of God's promise to Abraham; having been homeless for so many years, the Israelites are finally settled in a new home.*

# 106

1 Hallelujah!
   Give thanks to God, who is good,
      for God's mercy endures forever.
2 Who can declare the mighty acts of God
      or show forth all God's praise?

**antiphon**

3 Happy are those who act with justice
      and always do what is right!
4 Remember me, O God, with the favor you have for your people,
      and visit me with your saving help;
5    That I may see the prosperity of your elect
      and be glad with the gladness of your people,
      that I may glory with your inheritance.

**antiphon**

6 We have sinned as our ancestors did;
      we have done wrong and dealt wickedly.
7 In Egypt they did not consider your marvelous works,
      nor remember the abundance of your love;
      they defied the Most High at the Red Sea.
8 But God saved them for the Name's sake,
      to make God's power known.
9 God rebuked the Red Sea,
      and it dried up,
      and God led them through the deep as through a desert.
10 God saved them from the hand of those who hated them
      and redeemed them from the hand of the enemy.

11   The waters covered their oppressors;
         not one of them was left.
12   Then they believed God's words
         and sang songs of praise.

**antiphon**

13   But they soon forgot God's deeds
         and did not wait for God's counsel.
14   A craving seized them in the wilderness,
         and they put God to the test in the desert.
15   God gave them what they asked,
         then made them waste away.
16   They envied Moses in the camp,
         and Aaron, the holy one of God.
17   The earth opened and swallowed Dathan
         and covered the company of Abiram.
18   Fire blazed up against their company,
         and flames devoured the wicked.
19   Israel made a bull-calf at Horeb
         and worshiped a molten image;
20   And so they exchanged their Glory
         for the image of an ox that feeds on grass.

**antiphon**

21   They forgot God their Savior,
         who had done great things in Egypt,
22       wonderful deeds in the land of Ham,
         and fearful things at the Red Sea.
23   So God would have destroyed them,
         had not Moses, his chosen,
         stood in the breach,
         to turn away God's wrath from consuming them.
24   They refused the pleasant land
         and would not believe the promise.
25   They grumbled in their tents
         and would not listen to the voice of God.

**antiphon**

26 So God lifted a hand against them,
 to overthrow them in the wilderness,
27   to cast out their seed among the nations,
 and to scatter them throughout the lands.
28 They joined themselves to Baal-Peor
 and ate sacrifices offered to the dead.
29 They provoked God to anger with their actions,
 and a plague broke out among them.
30 Then Phinehas stood up and interceded,
 and the plague came to an end.
31 This was reckoned to him as righteousness
 throughout all generations forever.
32 They provoked God's anger at the waters of Meribah,
 so that Moses was punished because of them;
33   for they so embittered his spirit
 that he spoke rash words with his lips.

**antiphon**

34 They did not destroy the peoples
 as God had commanded them.
35   They intermingled with the heathen
 and learned their pagan ways,
36 So that they worshiped their idols,
 which became a snare to them.
37 They sacrificed their sons
 and their daughters to evil spirits.
38 They shed innocent blood,
 the blood of their sons and daughters,
 which they offered to the idols of Canaan,
 and the land was defiled with blood.
39 Thus they were polluted by their actions
 and went whoring in their evil deeds.

**antiphon**

40 Therefore God was angry with God's people
 and abhorred God's inheritance.
41 God gave them over to the hand of the heathen,
 and those who hated them ruled over them.

42 Their enemies oppressed them,
    and they were humbled under their hand.
43 Many a time did God deliver them,
    but they rebelled through their own devices,
    and were brought down in their iniquity.
44 Nevertheless, God saw their distress,
    and heard their lamentation.
45 God remembered the covenant with them
    and relented in accordance with great mercy.
46 God caused them to be pitied
    by those who held them captive.

**antiphon**

47 Save us, O God, our God,
    and gather us from among the nations,
    that we may give thanks to your holy Name
    and glory in your praise.

**antiphon**

48 Blessed be God, the God of Israel,
    From everlasting to everlasting;
    And let all the people say, "Amen!"
        Hallelujah!

**antiphon**

*Psalm 106 is a companion and contrast to Psalm 105. Although we have another historical psalm that tells the story of Israel, instead of focusing on how God has kept promises, it focuses on the sins of the people and their inability to keep their part of the covenant. Instead of ending with the Israelites finding a home in Jerusalem, it ends with them in the Babylonian exile, yearning for a second exodus.*

*Since these two psalms are so similar in content but so different in tone, I gave them the same antiphon, with slight variations. The words for each are taken from the last few verses of their respective psalms.*

# Book V

**107**

1  Give thanks to God, who is good,
     and God's mercy endures forever.
2  Let all those whom God has redeemed proclaim
     that they were redeemed from the hand of the foe.
3  God gathered them out of the lands;
     from the east and from the west,
     from the north and from the sea.
4  Some wandered in desert wastes;
     they found no way to a city
     where they might dwell.

5    Hungry and thirsty;
        their spirits languished.

**antiphon**

6    Then they cried to God in their trouble,
        and God delivered them from their distress.
7    God put their feet on a straight path
        to go to a city where they might dwell.
8    Let them give thanks to God for the mercy
        and wonders done for the children,
9        for God satisfies the thirsty
        and fills the hungry with good things.

**antiphon**

10   Some sat in darkness and deep gloom,
        bound fast in misery and iron
11      because they rebelled against the words of God
        and despised the counsel of the Most High.
12   So their spirits were humbled with hard labor;
        they stumbled, and there was none to help.
13   Then they cried to God in their trouble,
        and God delivered them from their distress.
14   God led them out of darkness and deep gloom
        and broke their bonds asunder.

**antiphon**

15   Let them give thanks to God for the mercy
        and wonders done for the children.
16      for God shatters the doors of bronze
        and breaks in two the iron bars.
17   Some were fools and took to rebellious ways;
        they were afflicted because of their sins.
18   They abhorred all manner of food
        and drew near to death's door.
19   Then they cried to God in their trouble,
        and were delivered from their distress.
20   God sent forth a word and healed them
        and saved them from the grave.

21  Let them give thanks to God for the mercy
        and wonders done for the children.
22  Let them offer a sacrifice of thanksgiving
        and tell of God's acts with shouts of joy.

**antiphon**

23  Some went down to the sea in ships
        and plied their trade in deep waters;
24      they beheld the works of God
        and the wonders of the deep.
25  Then God spoke, and a stormy wind arose,
        which tossed high the waves of the sea.
26  They mounted up to the heavens
        and fell back to the depths;
        their hearts melted because of their peril.
27      They reeled and staggered like drunkards
        and were at their wits' end.

**antiphon**

28  Then they cried to God in their trouble,
        and were delivered from their distress.
29  God stilled the storm to a whisper
        and quieted the waves of the sea.
30  Then were they glad because of the calm,
        and God brought them to the harbor they were bound for.
31  Let them give thanks to God for the mercy
        and wonders done for the children.
32  Let them exalt God in the congregation of the people
        and praise God in the council of the elders.

**antiphon**

33  God changed rivers into deserts,
        and water-springs into thirsty ground,
34      fruitful lands into salt flats,
        because of the wickedness of those who dwell there.
35  God changed deserts into pools of water
        and dry land into water-springs.
36  God settled the hungry there,
        and they founded a city to dwell in.

37 They sowed fields, and planted vineyards,
       and brought in a fruitful harvest.
38 God blessed them, so that they increased greatly;
       and did not let their herds decrease.
39     when they were diminished and brought low,
       through stress of adversity and sorrow.

**antiphon**

40 God pours contempt on princes
       and makes them wander in trackless wastes,
41     lifts the poor out of misery
       and multiplies their families like flocks of sheep.

**antiphon**

42 The upright will see this and rejoice,
       but all wickedness will shut its mouth.
43 Whoever is wise will ponder these things,
       and consider well the mercies of God.

**antiphon**

    *Book V begins with a thanksgiving for the end of the Babylonian exile, with each stanza dedicated to a different group in need of saving (desert wanderers, prisoners, the sick, and the shipwrecked) or, perhaps, different metaphors for the Exile. This is another psalm with two antiphons, one in verses 6, 13, 19, and 28, and the second in verses 8, 15, 21, and 31. I put both into counterpoint, along with the last concluding verse. If you can only do one part, do the bottom one—it stands on its own better than the other two.*

## 108    A Song. A Psalm of David.

1 My heart is firmly fixed, O God,
       I will sing and make melody.
   Wake up, my spirit!
2 Awake, lute and harp;
       I myself will waken the dawn.

3   I will confess you among the peoples, O God;
        I will sing praises to you among the nations.
4           For your loving-kindness is greater than the heavens,
        and your faithfulness reaches to the clouds.
5   Exalt yourself above the heavens, O God,
        and your glory over all the earth.
6   So that those who are dear to you may be delivered,
        save with your right hand and answer me.

**antiphon**

7   God spoke from the holy place and said,
        "I will exult and parcel out Shechem;
        I will divide the valley of Succoth.
8           Gilead is mine and Manasseh is mine;
        Ephraim is my helmet and Judah my scepter.
9           Moab is my washbasin,
        on Edom I throw down my sandal to claim it,
        and over Philistia will I shout in triumph."
10  Who will lead me into the strong city?
    Who will bring me into Edom?

**antiphon**

11  Have you not cast us off, O God?
        you no longer go out, O God, with our armies.
12  Grant us your help against the enemy,
        for vain is the help of humanity.
13  With God we will do valiant deeds,
        and shall tread our enemies under foot.

**antiphon**

*This is an interesting psalm because it demonstrates how the psalms were used, changed, redacted, and reimagined by different generations of worshipers (that or David was running out of ideas by this point in his career). The first five verses of the psalm are stolen from Psalm 57:7–11 and the last eight are stolen from Psalm 60:5–12. Although both are laments, Psalm 57 is an individual lament and Psalm 60 is a communal lament, leading to an abrupt shift in tone between verses 5 and 6. To reflect this, this antiphon uses the text of the fifty-seventh antiphon and the tune of the sixtieth antiphon.*

## 109  To the leader. Of David. A Psalm.

Do not be si - lent, O God of my praise.

1  O God of my praise,
    Hold not your tongue,
2      for the mouth of the wicked and deceitful,
    is opened against me.
3      They speak to me with a lying tongue;
  They encompass me with hateful words
    and fight against me without a cause.
4  Despite my love, they accuse me;
    but as for me, I pray for them.
5  They repay evil for good,
    and hatred for my love.

**antiphon**

6  They say, "Set the wicked against him,
    and let an accuser stand at his right hand;
7      when he is judged, let him be found guilty,
    and let his appeal be in vain.
8  Let his days be few,
    and let another take his office.
9  Let his children be fatherless,
    and his wife become a widow.
10  Let his children be waifs and beggars;
    let them be driven from the ruins of their homes.
11  Let the creditor seize everything he has;
    let strangers plunder his gains.

**antiphon**

12  Let there be no one to show him kindness,
    and none to pity his fatherless children,
13      let his descendants be destroyed,
    and his name be blotted out in the next generation.
14  Let the wickedness of his ancestors be remembered before God,
    and his mother's sin not be blotted out;

15 Let their sin be always before God;
>   but let him root out their names from the earth
16     because he did not remember to show mercy,
>   but persecuted the poor and needy
>   and sought to kill the brokenhearted.

**antiphon**

17 He loved cursing—let it come upon him;
>   he did not love blessing—let it depart from him.
18 He put on cursing like a garment,
>   let it soak into his body like water
>   and into his bones like oil;
19 Let it be to him like the cloak which he wraps around himself,
>   like the belt that he wears continually."
20 Let this be the recompense from God to my accusers,
>   and to those who speak evil against me.

**antiphon**

21 But you, O God my God,
>   oh, deal with me according to your Name;
> Good and faithful as you are, deliver me.
22 For I am poor and needy,
>   and my heart is wounded within me.
23 I have faded away like a shadow when it lengthens;
>   I am shaken off like a locust.
24 My knees are weak through fasting,
>   and my flesh is wasted and gaunt.
25 I have become a reproach to them;
>   they see and shake their heads.

**antiphon**

26 Help me, O God my God;
>   save me for your mercy's sake;
27     that they may know that this is your hand,
>   that you, O God, have done it.
28 They may curse, but you will bless;
>   let them rise but be put to shame,
>   and your servant will rejoice.

29 Let my accusers be clothed with disgrace
and wrap themselves in their shame as in a cloak.

**antiphon**

30 I will give great thanks to God with my mouth;
in the midst of the multitude will I praise him
31 because he stands at the right hand of the needy,
to save his life from those who would condemn him.

**antiphon**

*Here is another plea from someone falsely accused. Almost half of this psalm (vv. 6–19) is given over to quoting the curses and slanders of the psalmist's enemies, despite the fact that the psalmist has been praying for them (v. 4). The lengthy words of the "lying tongues" of the enemies are placed in contrast with God's silence.*

## 110   Of David. A Psalm.

1 God said to my ruler,
"Sit at my right hand,
until I make your enemies your footstool."

**antiphon**

2 God will send the scepter of your power out of Zion,
saying, "Rule over your enemies round about you.
3 Princely state has been yours
from the day of your birth
in the beauty of holiness have I begotten you,
like dew from the womb of the morning."

**antiphon**

4 God has sworn and will not recant:
"You are a priest forever after the order of Melchizedek."

5   God who is at your right hand
    God will smite rulers in the day of wrath;
6   God will rule over the nations.
        heaping high the corpses;
        smashing heads over the wide earth.
7   God will drink from the brook beside the road;
        with a head held high.

**antiphon**

*The author of the Epistle to the Hebrews quotes from this psalm quite a bit. The first verse is quoted in chapter 1 and the fourth is quoted in chapters 5 and 7. The epistle writer seems to believe that the psalms are God's utterances to Christ rather than humanity's utterances to God (or God's utterances to humanity). It is more likely that this is a royal psalm from the preexilic period, and there is no reason to give it special Christological significance. It's also not clear what the psalmist means by "by the order of Melchizedek"; this is the only place this mysterious figure is mentioned other than Genesis 14:18, and it's impossible to say what he meant to the ancient Israelites. Further confusing the issue is the fact that, in Hebrew, Melchizedek's name is* malki-tsedek (מַלְכִּי-צֶדֶק) *or "righteous king," so it would be just as possible to translate this verse as "You are a priest forever and a righteous king." This would make quite a bit of sense given that in the ancient Near East kings often had priestly functions.*

## 111

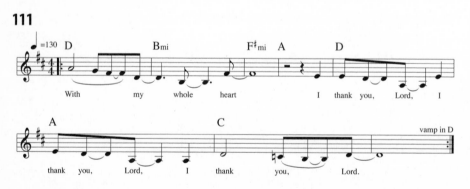

With my whole heart I thank you, Lord, I thank you, Lord, I thank you, Lord.

1   Hallelujah!
    I will give thanks to God with my whole heart,
        in the assembly of the upright, in the congregation.
2   Great are the deeds of God!
        they are studied by all who delight in them.
3   God's work is full of majesty and splendor,
        and God's righteousness endures forever.

4       God makes marvelous works to be remembered;
       God is gracious and full of compassion
5       and gives food to those who fear him;
       God is ever mindful of the covenant.
6   God has shown the people powerful works
       in giving them the lands of the nations.

**antiphon**

7   The works of God's hands are faithfulness and justice;
       all the commandments are sure,
8       standing fast forever and ever,
       wrought in truth and equity.
9   God sent redemption to the people;
       and commanded the covenant forever;
       holy and awesome is the Name.
10  The fear of God is the beginning of wisdom;
       those who act accordingly have a good understanding;
   God's praise endures forever.

**antiphon**

    *This psalm is an acrostic, probably used to help students learn the alphabet. It primarily focuses on praising God, although it borrows from wisdom literature in the last verse, possibly setting up Psalm 112, its sister psalm.*

    *This antiphon comes from Lacey Brown, the musician at Church of the Apostles, Seattle.*

## 112

1   Hallelujah!
    Happy are they who fear God
      and have great delight in the commandments!
2   Their descendants will be mighty in the land;
      the generation of the upright will be blessed.
3   Wealth and riches will be in their house,
      and their righteousness will last forever.

4   Light shines in the darkness for the upright;
       the righteous are merciful and full of compassion.
5   It is good for them to be generous in lending
       and to manage their affairs with justice.
6   For they will never be shaken;
       the righteous will be kept in everlasting remembrance.

**antiphon**

7   They will not be afraid of any evil rumors;
       their heart is right; they trust in God.
8   Their heart is established and will not shrink,
       until they see their desire upon their enemies.
9   They have given freely to the poor,
       and their righteousness stands fast forever;
       they will hold up their head with honor.
10  The wicked will see it and be angry;
       they will gnash their teeth and pine away;
       The desires of the wicked will perish.

**antiphon**

*Another acrostic psalm, 112 focuses more explicitly on the wisdom tradition. The first verse of Psalm 112 echoes the last verse of Psalm 111, focusing on the fear of God. While Psalm 111 focuses on the attributes of God, Psalm 112 focuses on the attributes of a godly people.*

## 113

Hal - le - lu - jah.   Hal - le - lu - jah.

Hal - le - lu - jah.   Hal - le - lu - jah.

1   Hallelujah!
    Give praise, you servants of God;
       praise the Name of God.

**antiphon**

2    Let the Name of God be blessed,
        from this time forth for evermore.
3    From the rising of the sun to its going down
        let the Name of God be praised.
4    God is high above all nations,
        and God's glory is above the heavens.
5    Who is like God, our God,
        who sits enthroned on high,
6        but sees what is below,
        the heavens and the earth?
7    God takes up the weak out of the dust
        and lifts up the poor from the ashes,
8        setting them with the rulers,
        with the rulers of the people.
9    God makes the woman of a childless house
        to be a joyful mother of children.
        Hallelujah.

**antiphon**

*Psalms 113–119 are referred to as the Hallel Psalms, and in the Jewish tradition they are prayed every morning in the Shacharit service. They are also prayed as part of the Passover meal, with Psalms 113 and 114 said before the meal and Psalms 115–118 said afterward. There's a good chance that Jesus sang this psalm at the Last Supper—see Matthew 26:30 and Mark 14:26.*

## 114

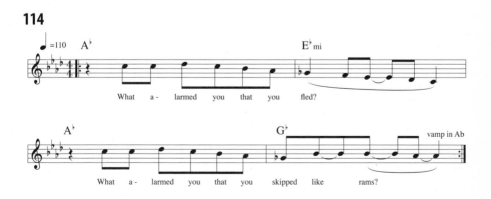

What a-larmed you that you fled?

What a-larmed you that you skipped like rams?

1    When Israel came out of Egypt,
         the house of Jacob from a people of strange speech,
2         Judah became a sanctuary
         and Israel a dominion.
3    The sea beheld it and fled;
         Jordan turned and went back,
4         the mountains skipped like rams,
         and the little hills like young sheep.
5    What ailed you, O sea, that you fled?
         O Jordan, that you turned back?
6         You mountains, that you skipped like rams?
         you little hills like young sheep?
7    Tremble, O Earth, at the presence of God,
         at the presence of the God of Jacob,
8         who turned the hard rock into a pool of water
         and flint into a flowing spring.

**antiphon**

    *It's noteworthy that God doesn't actually get a mention until the end of the psalm, when the presence of God is mentioned twice. Although it's obviously about the exodus, this psalm is traditionally read on Easter evening, which made me think of Mary Magdalene, Mary the mother of James, and Salome who fled from the tomb in terror when confronted with an angel announcing the resurrection of Christ. The oldest versions of Mark's gospel end with that moment, which means Mark thought it was important. Why did the women flee?*

## 115

    Not  to  us,  not  to  us,  but  to  your  name  give  glo - ry.
    *Lo  la - nu,  lo  la - nu,  ki  le - shim - kha  ten  ka - vod.*

1    Not to us, O God, not to us,
         but to your Name give glory;
         because of your love and because of your faithfulness.
2    Let not the nations say,
         "Where then is their God?"
3         when our God is in heaven
         doing whatever God wants.

218

4   Their idols are silver and gold,
        the work of human hands.
5   They have mouths, but cannot speak;
        eyes, but cannot see;
6         ears, but cannot hear;
        noses, but cannot smell;
7         hands, but cannot feel;
        feet, but cannot walk;
        they make no sound with their throat.
8   Those who fashion them
        all who put their trust in them,
        shall become like them.

**antiphon**

9   O Israel, trust in God;
    God is their help and their shield.
10  O house of Aaron, trust in God;
    God is their help and their shield.
11  You who fear God, trust in God,
        who is their help and their shield.

**antiphon**

12  God has been mindful of us.
    God will bless us.
        God will bless the house of Israel;
        and will bless the house of Aaron;
13         God will bless those who fear,
        both small and great together.

**antiphon**

14  May God increase you more and more,
        you and your children after you.
15  May you be blessed by God,
        the maker of heaven and earth.
16  The heaven of heavens is God's,
        but the earth is entrusted to its peoples.
17  The dead do not praise God,
        nor all those who go down into silence;

18    But we will bless God,
        from this time forth for evermore.
    Hallelujah!

**antiphon**

   *Given that so many psalms declare how much cooler Israel is than its neighbors, it's great to see this one start off with reminding us that it is God that is to be glorified, rather than us (or our nations). As John the Baptist said, "I must decrease so he may increase."*

   *Also, this psalm is a great example of how much musicality can be lost in the English translation. Although "not to us, not to us" nails the theme right on the head, it's just not as pretty as* lo lanu, lo lanu (לֹא לָנוּ, לֹא-לָנוּ). *Rather than trying to get the English to match the alliteration and consonance of the Hebrew, I just wrote a melody that would fit either and included both. I encourage you to try singing the Hebrew! Note that* kha *is guttural, like the "ch" in Bach, and* ten *is pronounced "tane." I love this psalm—it's a shame it didn't make it into the lectionary.*

## 116

1    I love God,
        for God hears my voice, my supplication
2        for God inclines an ear to me
        whenever I call.
3    The cords of death entangled me;
        the grip of the grave took hold of me;
    I came to grief and sorrow.
4        Then I called upon the Name of God:
        "O God, save my life."

**antiphon**

5    Gracious is God, and righteous;
        our God is full of compassion.

6    God watches over the innocent;
        I was brought very low, and God helped me.
7    Be at rest again, my soul.
        for God has treated you well.
8    For you have delivered me from death,
        my eyes from tears,
        my feet from stumbling.
9    I will walk in the presence of God
        in the land of the living.
10  I believed, even when I said,
        "I have been brought very low."
11      In my distress I said,
        "No one can be trusted."

**antiphon**

12  How shall I repay God
        for all the good things done for me?
13  I will lift up the cup of salvation
        and call upon the Name of God.
14  I will fulfill my vows to God
        in the presence of all people.
15  Precious in the sight of God
        is the death of servants.

**antiphon**

16  O God, I am your servant;
        I am your servant
        and the child of your handmaid;
        you have freed me from my bonds.
17  I will offer you the sacrifice of thanksgiving
        and call upon the Name of God.
18  I will fulfill my vows to God
        in the presence of all people,
19      in the courts of God's house,
        in the midst of you, O Jerusalem.
    Hallelujah!

**antiphon**

*I wrote this antiphon while doing a consultation in Connecticut with Trinity Wall Street. Bowie Snodgrass, Jonny Baker, and I threw together a service based on the Road to Emmaus. Bowie led us in a meditation, Jonny showed a hysterical biker safety clip about not seeing things that are right in front of you (go type "moonwalking bear" into YouTube), and I contributed this antiphon, which we sang over a heavy trip hop beat.*

## 117

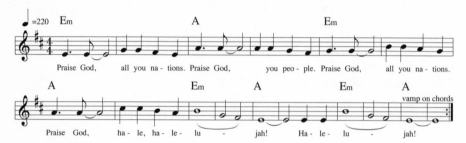

1   Praise God, all you nations;
        extol God, all you peoples,
2           for the loving-kindness toward us is great,
            and the faithfulness of God endures forever.
    Hallelujah!

**antiphon**

*For the shortest psalm in the Psalter, I thought it'd be good to write something that could really groove, and something that could be looped for a while. Just singing the antiphon, reading the psalm, and doing the antiphon again would probably take about thirty-five seconds, but it could become a full-on jam session with the right group. Folks with good ears will pick out harmonies easily, and the second half can be sung over the first to make counterpoint (like in "Seek Ye First").*

**118**

1   Give thanks to God, who is good;
        whose mercy endures forever.
2   Let Israel now proclaim,
        "God's mercy endures forever."
3   Let the house of Aaron now proclaim,
        "God's mercy endures forever."
4   Let those who fear God now proclaim,
        "God's mercy endures forever."

**antiphon**

5   I called to God in my distress;
        God answered by setting me free.
6   God is at my side,
        I will not fear;
        what can anyone do to me?
7   God is at my side to help me;
        I will triumph over those who hate me.

**antiphon**

8   It is better to rely on God
        than to put any trust in flesh.
9   It is better to rely on God
        than to put any trust in rulers.

**antiphon**

10  All the ungodly encompass me;
        in the Name of God I will repel them.

11   They hem me in, they hem me in on every side;
      in the name of God I will repel them.
12   They swarm about me like bees;
      they blaze like a fire of thorns;
      in the name of God I will repel them.

**antiphon**

13   I was pressed so hard
      that I almost fell,
      but God came to my help.
14   God is my strength and my song,
      and has become my salvation.
15   There is a sound of exultation and victory
      in the tents of the righteous:
"The right hand of God has triumphed!
16   The right hand of God is exalted!
The right hand of God has triumphed!"

**antiphon**

17   I shall not die, but live,
      and declare the works of God.
18   God has punished me sorely,
      but did not hand me over to death.

**antiphon**

19   Open for me the gates of righteousness;
      I will enter them and praise God.
20   "This is the gate of God;
      those who are righteous may enter."

**antiphon**

21   I will give thanks to you, for you answered me
      and have become my salvation.
22   The same stone which the builders rejected
      has become the chief cornerstone.
23   This is God's doing,
      and it is marvelous in our eyes.

24  This is the day that God has made;
       we will rejoice and be glad in it.
25  Hosanna, God, hosanna!
       God, send us now success.

**antiphon**

26  Blessed is the one who comes in the name of God;
       we bless you from the house of God.
27  God is God
       who has shined upon us;
       form a procession with branches up to the horns of the altar.
28  "You are my God, and I will thank you;
       you are my God, and I will exalt you."
29  Give thanks to God, who is good;
       whose mercy endures forever.

**antiphon**

*Since this thanksgiving psalm is the last of the Hallel Psalms and would conclude any recitation of them, I thought it should have some groove to it, which is where the bass line comes from.*

## 119  Aleph

1  Happy are they whose way is blameless,
       who walk in the law of God!
2  Happy are they who observe the decrees
       and seek God with all their hearts!
3  Who never do any wrong,
       but always walk in God's ways.

4    You laid down your commandments,
        that we should fully keep them.
5    Oh, that my ways were made so direct
        that I might keep your statutes!
6    Then I should not be put to shame,
        when I regard all your commandments.
7    I will thank you with an unfeigned heart,
        when I have learned your righteous judgments.
8    I will keep your statutes;
        do not utterly forsake me.

## 119  Beth

**antiphon**

9    How shall a young man cleanse his way?
        By keeping to your words.
10  With my whole heart I seek you;
        let me not stray from your commandments.
11  I treasure your promise in my heart,
        that I may not sin against you.
12  Blessed are you, O God;
        instruct me in your statutes.
13  With my lips will I recite
        all the judgments of your mouth.
14  I have taken greater delight in the way of your decrees
        than in all manner of riches.
15  I will meditate on your commandments
        and give attention to your ways;
16       my delight is in your statutes;
        I will not forget your word.

## 119 Gimel

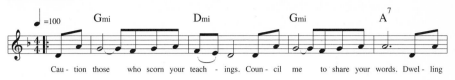

Cau - tion those who scorn your teach - ings. Coun - cil me to share your words. Dwel - ling

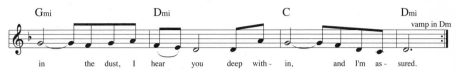

in the dust, I hear you deep with - in, and I'm as - sured.

17 Deal bountifully with your servant,
   that I may live and keep your word.
18 Open my eyes, that I may see
   the wonders of your law.
19 I am a stranger here on earth;
   do not hide your commandments from me.
20 My soul is consumed at all times
   with longing for your judgments.
21 You have rebuked the insolent;
   cursed are they who stray from your commandments!
22 Turn from me shame and rebuke,
   for I have kept your decrees.
23 Even though rulers sit and plot against me,
   I will meditate on your statutes.
24 For your decrees are my delight,
   and they are my counselors.


## 119 Daleth

**antiphon**

25 My soul cleaves to the dust;
   give me life according to your word.
26 I have confessed my ways, and you answered me;
   instruct me in your statutes.
27 Make me understand the way of your commandments,
   that I may meditate on your marvelous works.
28 I am wracked with grief;
   strengthen me according to your word.

29  Take from me the way of lying;
        let me find grace through your law.
30  I have chosen the way of faithfulness;
        I have set your judgments before me.
31  I hold fast to your decrees;
        O God, let me not be put to shame.
32  I will run the way of your commandments,
        for you have set my heart at liberty.

## 119  He

33  Teach me, O God, the way of your statutes,
        and I shall keep it to the end.
34  Give me understanding, and I shall keep your law;
        I shall keep it with all my heart.
35  Make me go in the path of your commandments,
        for that is my desire.
36  Incline my heart to your decrees
        and not to unjust gain.
37  Turn my eyes from watching what is worthless;
        give me life in your ways.
38  Fulfill your promise to your servant,
        which you make to those who fear you.
39  Turn away the reproach which I dread,
        because your judgments are good.
40  Behold, I long for your commandments;
        in your righteousness preserve my life.

## 119 Vav

**antiphon**

41  Let your loving-kindness come to me, O God,
      and your salvation, according to your promise.
42  Then shall I have a word for those who taunt me,
      because I trust in your words.
43  Do not take the word of truth out of my mouth,
      for my hope is in your judgments.
44  I shall continue to keep your law;
      I shall keep it forever and ever.
45  I will walk at liberty,
      because I study your commandments.
46  I will tell of your decrees before kings
      and will not be ashamed.
47  I delight in your commandments,
      which I have always loved.
48  I will lift up my hands to your commandments,
      and I will meditate on your statutes.

## 119 Zayin

49  Remember your word to your servant,
      because you have given me hope.
50  This is my comfort in my trouble,
      that your promise gives me life.
51  The proud have derided me cruelly,
      but I have not turned from your law.
52  When I remember your judgments of old,
      O God, I take great comfort.

53 I am filled with a burning rage,
    because of the wicked who forsake your law.
54 Your statutes have been like songs to me
    wherever I have lived as a stranger.
55 I remember your Name in the night, O God,
    and dwell upon your law.
56 This is how it has been with me,
    because I have kept your commandments.

## 119 Heth

**antiphon**

57 You only are my portion, O God;
    I have promised to keep your words.
58 I entreat you with all my heart,
    be merciful to me according to your promise.
59 I have considered my ways
    and turned my feet toward your decrees.
60 I hasten and do not tarry
    to keep your commandments.
61 Though the cords of the wicked entangle me,
    I do not forget your law.
62 At midnight I will rise to give you thanks,
    because of your righteous judgments.
63 I am a companion of all who fear you
    and of those who keep your commandments.
64 The earth, O God, is full of your love;
    instruct me in your statutes.

## 119 Teth

65 O God, you have dealt graciously with your servant,
      according to your word.
66 Teach me discernment and knowledge,
      for I have believed in your commandments.
67 Before I was afflicted I went astray,
      but now I keep your word.
68 You are good and you bring forth good;
      instruct me in your statutes.
69 The proud have smeared me with lies,
      but I will keep your commandments with my whole heart.
70 Their heart is gross and fat,
      but my delight is in your law.
71 It is good for me that I have been afflicted,
      that I might learn your statutes.
72 The law of your mouth is dearer to me
      than thousands in gold and silver.

## 119 Yod

**antiphon**

73 Your hands have made me and fashioned me;
      give me understanding, that I may learn your commandments.
74 Those who fear you will be glad when they see me,
      because I trust in your word.
75 I know, O God, that your judgments are right
      and that in faithfulness you have afflicted me.
76 Let your loving-kindness be my comfort,
      as you have promised to your servant.

77 Let your compassion come to me, that I may live,
  for your law is my delight.
78 Let the arrogant be dismayed, for they wrong me with lies;
  but I will meditate on your commandments.
79 Let those who fear you turn to me,
  and also those who know your decrees.
80 Let my heart be sound in your statutes,
  that I may not be put to shame.

## 119 Kaph

Kin-dle me with strength and pa - - tience. Keep me from the an-gry throng! Like the moun- tains as you raised them, lift me up and hold me strong.

81 I long for your deliverance;
  I have put my hope in your word.
82 My eyes have failed from watching for your promise,
  and I say, "When will you comfort me?"
83 I have become like a leather flask in the smoke,
  but I have not forgotten your statutes.
84 How much longer must I wait?
  when will you give judgment against those who persecute me?
85 The proud have dug pits for me;
  they do not keep your law.
86 All your commandments are true;
  help me, for they persecute me with lies.
87 They had almost made an end of me on earth,
  but I have not forsaken your commandments.
88 In your loving-kindness, revive me,
  that I may keep the decrees of your mouth.

## 119  Lamedh

antiphon

89  O God, your word is everlasting;
      it stands firm in the heavens.
90  Your faithfulness remains from one generation to another;
      you established the earth, and it abides.
91  By your decree these continue to this day,
      for all things are your servants.
92  If my delight had not been in your law,
      I should have perished in my affliction.
93  I will never forget your commandments,
      because by them you give me life.
94  I am yours; oh, that you would save me!
      for I study your commandments.
95  Though the wicked lie in wait for me to destroy me,
      I will apply my mind to your decrees.
96  I see that all things come to an end,
      but your commandment has no bounds.

## 119  Mem

Mind-ful of your truth in-side me, med-i-tate with ev-ery breath need-ing on-ly you to guide me nev-er turn-ing from your path.

97  Oh, how I love your law!
All the day long it is in my mind!
98  Your commandment has made me wiser than my enemies,
      and it is always with me.
99  I have more understanding than all my teachers,
      for your decrees are my study.
100  I am wiser than the elders,
      because I observe your commandments.

101 I restrain my feet from every evil way,
      that I may keep your word.
102 I do not shrink from your judgments,
      because you yourself have taught me.
103 How sweet are your words to my taste!
      they are sweeter than honey to my mouth.
104 Through your commandments I gain understanding;
      therefore I hate every lying way.

# 119 Nun

## antiphon

105 Your word is a lantern to my feet
      and a light upon my path.
106 I have sworn and am determined
      to keep your righteous judgments.
107 I am deeply troubled;
      preserve my life, O God, according to your word.
108 Accept, O God, the willing tribute of my lips,
      and teach me your judgments.
109 My life is always in my hand,
      yet I do not forget your law.
110 The wicked have set a trap for me,
      but I have not strayed from your commandments.
111 Your decrees are my inheritance forever;
      truly, they are the joy of my heart.
112 I have applied my heart to fulfill your statutes
      forever and to the end.

## 119 Samekh

Oth - ers try, with lies en - snare me. On - ly you can get me through. Pass - ing

through my plight and pe - ril, per - se - vere for love of you.

113 I hate those who have a divided heart,
      but your law do I love.
114 You are my refuge and shield;
      my hope is in your word.
115 Away from me, you wicked!
      I will keep the commandments of my God.
116 Sustain me according to your promise, that I may live,
      and let me not be disappointed in my hope.
117 Hold me up, and I shall be safe,
      and my delight shall be ever in your statutes.
118 You spurn all who stray from your statutes;
      their deceitfulness is in vain.
119 In your sight all the wicked of the earth are but dross;
      therefore I love your decrees.
120 My flesh trembles with dread of you;
      I am afraid of your judgments.

## 119 Ayin

**antiphon**

121 I have done what is just and right;
      do not deliver me to my oppressors.
122 Be surety for your servant's good;
      let not the proud oppress me.
123 My eyes have failed from watching for your salvation
      and for your righteous promise.
124 Deal with your servant according to your loving-kindness
      and teach me your statutes.

125 I am your servant; grant me understanding,
      that I may know your decrees.
126 It is time for you to act, O God,
      for they have broken your law.
127 Truly, I love your commandments
      more than gold and precious stones.
128 I hold all your commandments to be right for me;
      all paths of falsehood I abhor.

## 119  Pe

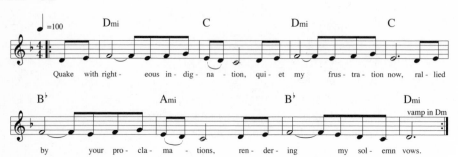

Quake with righteous indignation, quiet my frustration now, rallied by your proclamations, rendering my solemn vows.

129 Your decrees are wonderful;
      therefore I obey them with all my heart.
130 When your word goes forth it gives light;
      it gives understanding to the simple.
131 I open my mouth and pant;
      I long for your commandments.
132 Turn to me in mercy,
      as you always do to those who love your Name.
133 Steady my footsteps in your word;
      let no iniquity have dominion over me.
134 Rescue me from those who oppress me,
      and I will keep your commandments.
135 Let your countenance shine upon your servant
      and teach me your statutes.
136 My eyes shed streams of tears,
      because people do not keep your law.

## 119  Sadhe

antiphon

137  You are righteous, O God,
      and upright are your judgments.
138  You have issued your decrees
      with justice and in perfect faithfulness.
139  My indignation has consumed me,
      because my enemies forget your words.
140  Your word has been tested to the uttermost,
      and your servant holds it dear.
141  I am small and of little account,
      yet I do not forget your commandments.
142  Your justice is an everlasting justice
      and your law is the truth.
143  Trouble and distress have come upon me,
      yet your commandments are my delight.
144  The righteousness of your decrees is everlasting;
      grant me understanding, that I may live.

## 119  Qoph

Save your ser- vant ev - er faith - ful. Take me from this place of pain. Un - der

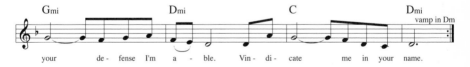

your de - fense I'm a - ble. Vin - di - cate me in your name.

145  I call with my whole heart;
      answer me, O God,
      that I may keep your statutes.
146  I call to you; save me!
      I will keep your decrees.
147  Early in the morning I cry out to you,
      for in your word is my trust.

148 My eyes are open in the night watches,
  that I may meditate upon your promise.
149 Hear my voice, O God, according to your loving-kindness;
  according to your judgments, give me life.
150 They draw near who in malice persecute me;
  they are very far from your law.
151 You, O God, are near at hand,
  and all your commandments are true.
152 Long have I known from your decrees
  that you have established them forever.

## 119   Resh

**antiphon**

153 Behold my affliction and deliver me,
  for I do not forget your law.
154 Plead my cause and redeem me;
  according to your promise, give me life.
155 Deliverance is far from the wicked,
  for they do not study your statutes.
156 Great is your compassion, O God;
  preserve my life, according to your judgments.
157 There are many who persecute and oppress me,
  yet I have not swerved from your decrees.
158 I look with loathing at the faithless,
  for they have not kept your word.
159 See how I love your commandments!
  O God, in your mercy, preserve me.
160 The heart of your word is truth;
  all your righteous judgments endure for evermore.

## 119 Shin

161 Rulers have persecuted me without a cause,
　　but my heart stands in awe of your word.

162 I am as glad because of your promise
　　as one who finds great spoils.

163 As for lies, I hate and abhor them,
　　but your law is my love.

164 Seven times a day do I praise you,
　　because of your righteous judgments.

165 Great peace have they who love your law.
　　For them there is no stumbling block.

166 I have hoped for your salvation, O God,
　　and have fulfilled your commandments.

167 I have kept your decrees
　　and I have loved them deeply.

168 I have kept your commandments and decrees,
　　for all my ways are before you.


## 119　Tav

**antiphon**

169 Let my cry come before you, O God;
　　give me understanding, according to your word.

170 Let my supplication come before you;
　　deliver me, according to your promise.

171 My lips shall pour forth your praise,
　　when you teach me your statutes.

172 My tongue shall sing of your promise,
　　for all your commandments are righteous.

173 Let your hand be ready to help me,
    for I have chosen your commandments.
174 I long for your salvation, O God,
    and your law is my delight.
175 Let me live, and I will praise you,
    and let your judgments help me.
176 I have gone astray like a sheep that is lost;
    search for your servant,
    for I do not forget your commandments.

**antiphon**

*These antiphons, when sung end-to-end, form a hymn. See pages 20-21 for details.*

## 120   A Song of Ascents.

I am for peace, but when I speak, they are for war.

1   When I was in trouble, I called to God;
    and was answered.
2   Deliver me, O God, from lying lips
    and from the deceitful tongue.
3   What can you profit,
        and what more besides,
        O you deceitful tongue?
4   The sharpened arrows of a warrior,
    along with hot glowing coals.

**antiphon**

5   How hateful it is that I must lodge in Meshech
    and dwell among the tents of Kedar!
6   Too long have I had to live among the enemies of peace.
7   I am on the side of peace,
        but when I speak of it,
        they are for war.

**antiphon**

Psalms 120–134 form a collection called "Songs of Ascent," which probably originated as songs to be sung by pilgrims on their way to Zion. I've tried to write the antiphons so that they sound natural at walking tempo (for many of them, you'll want to walk in half-time to prevent your procession from scuttling down the aisle). In modern usage, the Eastern Orthodox church sings them as a group every weeknight during Lent. Try using them for a Lenten processional.

## 121   A Song of Ascents.

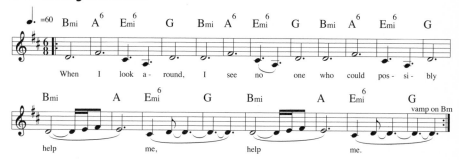

1   I lift up my eyes to the hills;
        from where is my help to come?
2   My help comes from God,
        the maker of heaven and earth.
3   God will not let your foot be moved
        and the one who watches over you will not fall asleep.
4   Behold, the one who keeps watch over Israel
        shall neither slumber nor sleep;
5   God himself watches over you;
        God is your shade
        at your right hand,
6   So that the sun shall not strike you by day,
        nor the moon by night.
7   God shall preserve you from all evil;
        and shall keep you safe.
8   God shall guard your going out and your coming in,
        from this time forth and for evermore.

**antiphon**

We have another contribution from Lacey Brown. When folks who like my music ask me if there are other, similar artists they should check, Lacey is always near the top of my lists. You should check her out, too: http://www.laceybrown.com/.

241

*The reason I never wrote an antiphon for this psalm is that whenever it comes up in worship (which it does frequently), we use the chorus from John Lennon's "Help!" which makes a surprisingly good antiphon.*

## 122   A Song of Ascents. Of David.

Be - cause   of  the  house  of  the  Lord   our  God,   I  will  seek   to  do  you  good.

1   I was glad when they said to me,
       "Let us go to the house of God."
2   Now our feet are standing within your gates, O Jerusalem.
3       Jerusalem is built as a city that is at unity with itself;
4       To which the tribes make pilgrimage,
         the tribes of God,
         the assembly of Israel,
         to praise the Name of God.
5   For there are the thrones of judgment,
         the thrones of the house of David.

**antiphon**

6   Pray for the peace of Jerusalem:
       "May they prosper who love you.
7   Peace be within your walls
       and quietness within your towers.
8   For my brethren and companions' sake,
       I pray for your prosperity
9       because of the house of God, our God,
       I will seek to do you good."

**antiphon**

*This is the only Psalm of Ascent that is plainly about pilgrimage to Jerusalem. It's worth noting that Psalm 120 (a psalm about living among strangers) leads into Psalm 121 (a psalm about protection for a journey), which leads into Psalm 122 (a psalm about arriving at the Temple in Jerusalem and living in peace among friends).*

## 123  A Song of Ascents.

Have mer - cy on us. Have mer - cy on us.
Kha - ne - nu, A - do - nai. Kha - ne - nu, A - do - nai.

1  To you, I lift up my eyes,
      to you, enthroned in the heavens.
2  As the eyes of servants look to the hand of their masters,
      and the eyes of a maid to the hand of her mistress,
      so our eyes look to you, our God,
      awaiting favor.
3  Have mercy upon us, O God,
      have mercy!
   We have had more than enough of contempt,
4  Too long have we endured
      the scorn of the indolent rich,
      the derision of the proud.

**antiphon**

*The thing I love about the Psalms of Ascent is that they're so simple and so short, yet they say everything they need to say. This is even more pronounced in the original Hebrew, in which none of these lines are longer than four or five words. I wish I could reproduce the whole thing, but since I can't, I'll just include the Hebrew in the antiphon.*

## 124  A Song of Ascents. Of David.

The snare is bro - ken and we have es - caped.  Bless - ed be our God!

1  If God had not been on our side,
      let Israel now say;
2  If God had not been on our side,
      when enemies rose up against us;
3  then would they have swallowed us up alive
      in their fierce anger toward us;
4  Then would the waters have overwhelmed us
      and the torrent gone over us;

243

5       Then would the raging waters
          have gone right over us.

6    Blessed be God, who did not give us
          over to be a prey for their teeth.

7    We have escaped like a bird from the snare of the fowler;
          the snare is broken, and we have escaped.

8    Our help is in the Name of God,
          the maker of heaven and earth.

**antiphon**

     *In the lectionary, this psalm is paired with the moment when Esther convinces King Ahasuerus to keep Haman from killing the Jews (Esther 7). I felt that the melody needed to be cheerful enough to sing on Purim, although I always wished that the story ended on a less vindictive note. . . .*

## 125   A Song of Ascents.

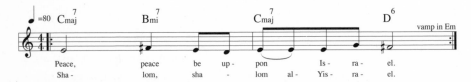

1    Those who trust in God
         are like Mount Zion,
         which cannot be moved,
         but stands fast forever.

2    The hills stand about Jerusalem;
         so does God stand round about the people,
         from this time forth and for evermore.

3       The scepter of the wicked shall never rest
         upon land allotted to the just,
         that the just shall not put their hands to evil.

4    Show your goodness, O God, to those who are good
         and to those who are true of heart.

5    As for those who turn aside to crooked ways,
         God will lead them away with the evildoers;
    Peace be upon Israel.

**antiphon**

*Jerusalem is not exactly a peaceful place today, nor was it in the time of Jesus, or just about any other time for that matter. The idea of God enveloping the people of Jerusalem like the mountains that surround it is a lovely thought, but a difficult one to believe. As I wrote this, I was watching two monks get into a fistfight in the middle of the Church of the Holy Sepulchre on CNN, which broke my heart.*

## 126   A Song of Ascents.

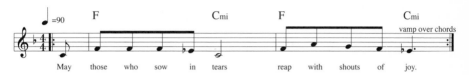

May those who sow in tears reap with shouts of joy.

1    When God restored the fortunes of Zion,
           then were we like those who dream.
2           our mouths filled with laughter,
           and our tongues with shouts of joy.
        Then they said among the nations,
           "God has done great things for them."
3    God has done great things for us,
           and we are glad indeed.

**antiphon**

4    Restore our fortunes, O God,
           like the watercourses of the Negeb.
5    Those who sowed with tears
           will reap with songs of joy.
6    Those who go out weeping,
           carrying the seed,
           will come again with joy,
           shouldering their sheaves.

**antiphon**

*It's interesting that this psalm begins by recounting what happened when God restored the fortunes of the community, but ends by imploring God to . . . restore the fortunes of the community. It's as if the community is so confident in God's deliverance that it's giving thanks and praising God in advance. Or, perhaps, these two stanzas refer to different periods in the community's history, which implies that not all restoration is permanent and that current prosperity and joy don't guarantee the future.*

## 127  A Song of Ascents. Of Solomon.

Un - less God builds a house, its build - ers work in vain.

1    Unless God builds the house,
          in vain the builders labor.
          Unless God watches over the city,
          in vain the watchman keeps vigil.
2    It is in vain that you rise so early
          and go to bed so late;
          vain, too, to eat the bread of toil,
          for God gives sleep to the beloved.

**antiphon**

3    Children are a heritage from God,
          and the fruit of the womb is a gift.
4    Like arrows in the hand of a warrior
          are the children of one's youth.
5    Happy are they who have a quiver full of them!
          they shall not be put to shame
          when they contend with enemies at the gate.

**antiphon**

*I spent a lot of time with this psalm when Transmission was first getting started. Planting a new church is a lot of work and can be very discouraging. It's also easy to become so wrapped up in your own work that you forget to stay focused on God's work. This is a psalm for anyone starting a new project.*

*Also, verse 4 is probably the inspiration for Khalil Gibran's "On Children" from The Prophet. It's a remarkable book—check it out if you haven't already.*

## 128　A Song of Ascents.

Blessed are they who walk in the way of God.

1　Happy are they all who fear God,
　　and who follow in God's ways!
2　You shall eat the fruit of your labor;
　　happiness and prosperity shall be yours.
3　Your beloved shall be like a fruitful vine within your house,
　　your children like olive shoots round about your table.
4　The one who fears God shall thus indeed be blessed.

**antiphon**

5　God bless you from Zion,
　　may you see the prosperity of Jerusalem
　　all the days of your life,
6　　and may you live to see your children's children;
　　Peace be upon Israel.

**antiphon**

*Here we have a portrait of ideal family life, albeit from a man's perspective. Like a few of the other Psalms of Ascent, this one ends with a prayer for Israel. Maybe there's some connection between strong families and strong communities?*

## 129　A Song of Ascents.

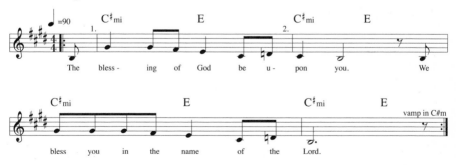

The bless - ing of God be u - pon you. We

bless you in the name of the Lord.

1　"Greatly have they oppressed me since my youth,"
　　let Israel now say;

2    "Greatly have they oppressed me since my youth,
     but they have not prevailed against me."
3    The plowmen plowed upon my back
     and made their furrows long.
4    God, the Righteous One,
     has cut the cords of the wicked.

**antiphon**

5    Let all those who are enemies of Zion
     fall back in disgrace.
6    Let them be like grass upon the housetops,
     which withers before it can be plucked,
7    which does not fill the hand of the reaper,
     no armful for the gatherer of sheaves,
8    so that passersby say not so much as,
     "God prosper you.
     We wish you well in the Name of God."

**antiphon**

*The final blessing (v. 8b), which seems to be common practice between reapers, is quite probably connected to the one found in Ruth 2:4, when Boaz blesses the people working his fields. It's also quite similar to the opening of the Sursum Corda, and this melody would be a nice way to start a eucharistic prayer. It could be done as a call and response in which the celebrant sings the first line and the congregation responds with the second, or the entire antiphon can be done as a round, enabling two parts of the congregation to bless each other while singing.*

## 130   A Song of Ascents.

1    Out of the depths I called to you, O God;

2        God, hear my voice;
        let your ears consider well
        the voice of my supplication.

3    If you, God, were to note what is done amiss,
        O God, who could stand?

4    For there is forgiveness with you;
        therefore you shall be feared.

**antiphon**

5    I wait for God;
        with my entire being, I wait for God;
        whose word is my hope.

6    I am eager for God,
        more than watchmen for the morning,
        more than watchmen for the morning.

**antiphon**

7    O Israel, wait for God,
        for with God there is mercy;

8        and great power for redemption,
    God shall redeem Israel from all its sins.

**antiphon**

While Psalm 129 is asking for deliverance from Israel's enemies, Psalm 130 is asking for redemption for Israel's iniquities. These two Psalms of Ascent balance each other nicely. There are lots and lots of brilliant settings of this psalm, but I'd recommend checking out Sinéad O'Connor's "Out of the Depths" from her album Theology. It's very singable and would work well in church.

For those keeping track, 130 is the sixth Penitential Psalm.

## 131  A Song Ascents. Of David.

I have taught my-self to be con-tent. I am like a child with its mo-ther.

1    O God, I am not proud;
         I have no haughty looks.
         I do not occupy myself with great matters,
         or with things that are too hard for me.

2        But I have taught myself to be contented,
         like a child upon its mother's breast;
         like a weaned child am I.

3    O Israel, wait upon God,
         from this time forth and for evermore.

**antiphon**

*This is one of the few psalms that seems like it was written by a woman and, per-haps not coincidentally, it's one of the few places in the Bible that uses a maternal im-age for God. It's a shame that it's only used once in the lectionary, on the eighth week of Epiphany in Year A, and only when there are at least a full eight weeks between Epiphany and Lent, which isn't often.*

## 132  A Song of Ascents.

I will not rest un-til I find a place for the Might-y One.

1    God, remember David,
         and all the hardships he endured;

2        how he swore an oath to God,
         vowing to the Mighty One of Jacob:

3        "I will not come under the roof of my house,
         nor climb up into my bed;

4        I will not allow my eyes to sleep,
         nor let my eyelids slumber

5        until I find a place for God,
         a dwelling for the Mighty One of Jacob."

6    "The ark! We heard it was in Ephratah;
         we found it in the fields of Jearim.
7    Let us go to the dwelling place of God;
         let us fall upon our knees before the footstool."
8    Arise, O God, into your resting-place,
         you and the ark of your strength.
9    Let your priests be clothed with righteousness;
         let your faithful people sing with joy.
10   For your servant David's sake,
         do not turn away the face of your Anointed.
11   God has sworn an oath to David in truth,
         and will not break it:
         "I set upon your throne a child, the fruit of your body.
12   If your children keep my covenant
         and my testimonies that I teach them,
         their children
         will sit upon your throne
         for evermore."

**antiphon**

13   For God has chosen Zion;
         and has desired her for a habitation:
14   "This shall be my resting-place for ever;
         here will I dwell, for I delight in her.
15   I will surely bless her provisions,
         and satisfy her poor with bread.
16   I will clothe her priests with salvation,
         and her faithful people will rejoice and sing.
17   There will I make the horn of David flourish;
         I have prepared a lamp for my Anointed.
18   As for David's enemies, I will clothe them with shame;
         but as for him, his crown will shine."

**antiphon**

   *Continuing with the pilgrimage theme, this psalm hearkens back to 2 Samuel 7, when David wanted to build a temple for God but Nathan the prophet told him not to. When Solomon finally did build a temple, he concluded his prayer of dedication by quoting verses 8–9 of this psalm (2 Chronicles 6).*

## 133  A Song of Ascents.

How good  it  is  when  kin  live to- geth- er  in  har- mo- ny.

1    Oh, how good and pleasant it is,
        when kindred live together in unity!
2    It is like fine oil upon the head
        that runs down upon the beard,
        upon the beard of Aaron,
        and runs down upon the collar of his robe,
3        like the dew of Hermon
        that falls upon the hills of Zion.
    There the God has ordained the blessing:
        life for evermore.

**antiphon**

*This is a prayer for national unity (or, perhaps, reunification). Mount Hermon is an important mountain in the north (the Kingdom of Israel) and Mount Zion, of course, is Jerusalem in the south (the Kingdom of Judah). This is a good prayer for the day after an election.*

## 134  A Song of Ascents.

Bless  God,  you  ser - vants  of  God,  who  stand  through  the  night  in  the  house  of  God.

1    Behold now, praise God,
        you servants of God,
        who stand through the night
        in the house of God.
2    Lift up your hands in the holy place
        and praise God;
3    May the one who made heaven and earth
        bless you out of Zion.

**antiphon**

*Like many of the Psalms of Ascent, this little psalm seemed too short to warrant an antiphon. Could I really expect people to repeat the antiphon after every verse? Probably not, so I decided to write it as a round. I imagine this working really well at vigils, lock-ins, and all-night protests, so I wrote it to be guitar-friendly. The melody is robust enough to work without accompaniment when it's sung as a three-part round. It should be sung confidently with a strong pulse on one and three.*

## 135

Praise God, whose name en - dures for - ev - er.

1 Hallelujah!
Praise the Name of God;
    give praise, you servants of God.
2     who stand in the house of God,
    in the courts of the house of our God.
3 Praise God, who is good;
    sing praises to the Name, for it is lovely.
4 For God has chosen Jacob
    and Israel as a treasured possession.

**antiphon**

5 For I know that God is great,
    and that our sovereign is above all gods.
6 God does what God wants,
    in heaven and on earth,
    in the seas and all the deeps.
7 God brings up rain clouds from the ends of the earth;
    and sends out lightning with the rain,
    and brings the winds out the vaults.
8 It was God who struck down the firstborn of Egypt,
    both human and beast.
9 God sent signs and wonders into the midst of you, O Egypt,
    against Pharaoh and all his servants,
10     and overthrew many nations,
    putting mighty kings to death:

11      Sihon, king of the Amorites,
        and Og, the kingdoms of Bashan,
        and all the kings of Canaan,
12     and gave their land to be an inheritance,
        an inheritance for Israel, God's people.

**antiphon**

13  O God, your Name is everlasting;
        your renown, O God, endures from age to age,
14     for God gives people justice
        and shows compassion to servants.

**antiphon**

15  The idols of the heathen are silver and gold,
        the work of human hands.
16  They have mouths, but cannot speak;
        eyes, but cannot see.
17     ears, but cannot hear;
        nor is there any breath in their mouths.
18  Those who make them,
        and those who trust in them,
        shall be like them.

**antiphon**

19  Bless God, O house of Israel;
        O house of Aaron, bless God.
20     Bless God, O house of Levi;
        you who fear God, bless God.
21  Blessed be God out of Zion,
        who dwells in Jerusalem.
        Hallelujah!

**antiphon**

    *Like the psalm that follows it, Psalm 135 gives a CliffsNotes version of the Torah, from creation to Jacob to the exodus to the conquest of Canaan, thereby emphasizing God's continuity through the ages.*

## 136

whose stead - fast love is e - ter - nal.

1   Give thanks to God, who is good,
     **whose steadfast love is eternal.**
2   Give thanks to the God of gods,
     **whose steadfast love is eternal.**
3   Give thanks to the Lord of lords,
     **whose steadfast love is eternal.**
4   Who only does great wonders,
     **whose steadfast love is eternal;**
5   Who by wisdom made the heavens,
     **whose steadfast love is eternal;**
6   Who spread out the earth upon the waters,
     **whose steadfast love is eternal;**
7   Who created great lights,
     **whose steadfast love is eternal;**
8   The sun to rule the day,
     **whose steadfast love is eternal;**
9   The moon and the stars to govern the night,
     **whose steadfast love is eternal.**
10  Who struck down the firstborn of Egypt,
     **whose steadfast love is eternal;**
11  And brought out Israel from among them,
     **whose steadfast love is eternal;**
12  With a mighty hand and a stretched-out arm,
     **whose steadfast love is eternal;**
13  Who divided the Red Sea in two,
     **whose steadfast love is eternal;**
14  And made Israel to pass through the midst of it,
     **whose steadfast love is eternal;**
15  But swept Pharaoh and his army into the Red Sea,
     **whose steadfast love is eternal;**
16  Who led his people through the wilderness,
     **whose steadfast love is eternal.**
17  Who struck down great kings,
     **whose steadfast love is eternal;**

18  And slew mighty kings,
    **whose steadfast love is eternal;**
19  Sihon, king of the Amorites,
    **whose steadfast love is eternal;**
20  And Og, the king of Bashan,
    **whose steadfast love is eternal;**
21  And gave away their lands for an inheritance,
    **whose steadfast love is eternal;**
22  An inheritance for Israel, God's servant,
    **whose steadfast love is eternal.**
23  Who remembered us in our low estate,
    **whose steadfast love is eternal;**
24  And delivered us from our enemies,
    **whose steadfast love is eternal;**
25  Who gives food to all creatures,
    **whose steadfast love is eternal.**
26  Give thanks to the God of heaven,
    **whose steadfast love is eternal.**

*This is another example of an antiphon being preserved in the Psalter, ready for use. Unlike most psalms in this book, I'd recommend using the antiphon after every verse—I kept the melody short and simple for just that reason. The two bars of rest are there to give the reader a chance to shout out the first half of each verse, allowing the second half to be sung by the congregation. This psalm should be done with a lot of energy, preferably with lots of drums and a bonfire.*

## 137

How can we sing your song in a fo-reign land?

1       By the waters of Babylon
        we sat down and wept,
        when we remembered Zion.
2       There on the poplars
        we hung up our harps
3       for our captors asked us for a song,
        our oppressors called for mirth:
        "Sing us one of the songs of Zion."

4   How shall we sing a song of God
        in a strange land?
5   If I forget you, O Jerusalem,
        let my right hand wither.
6   Let my tongue cleave to the roof of my mouth
        if I do not remember you,
        if I do not set Jerusalem
        above my highest joy.

**antiphon**

7   Remember the day of Jerusalem, O God,
        against the people of Edom,
        who said, "Strip her, strip her
        even to the ground!"
8   O Daughter of Babylon, predator,
        blessed be the one who pays you back
        for what you have done to us!
9   Blessed be the one who takes your little ones,
        and dashes them against rocks!

**antiphon**

*There is no shortage of great settings of this psalm, although my favorite by far is the 1972 reggae version by The Melodians (although the covers by Sublime and Sinéad O'Connor are great, too). Also check out "Jerusalem" by Matisyahu, which relies on verses 5–6 for its chorus. I'd be remiss if I didn't also mention "On the Willows" from* Godspell, *although musical theatre has never really been my thing.*

*Perhaps unsurprisingly, most settings of this psalm omit the last verse; somehow, "O, Babylon, blessed are they who take your babies and dash them on rocks" doesn't seem appropriately worshipful. Since there are so many alternative settings of this psalm already, I considered using that verse since no one ever has, but honestly it seems as if verse 4 is a much better summary of the entire psalm. Still, I hope congregations won't pretend that verse doesn't exist, but rather address it directly and consider how we deal with our anger against our tormenters.*

## 138  Of David.

They shall sing of the ways of the Lord, "Great is the glo - ry of God!"

1   I praise you with my whole heart;
     before the divine beings I sing to you.
2   I will bow down toward your holy temple
     and praise your Name, because of your love and faithfulness,
     for you have glorified your Name, your word, above all things.
3   When I called, you answered me;
     you gave me strength.

**antiphon**

4   All the rulers of the earth will praise you, O God,
     when they have heard the words of your mouth.
5   They will sing of your ways,
     that great is your glory.
6   Though you are high, you care for the lowly;
     and perceive the haughty from afar.

**antiphon**

7   Though I walk in the midst of trouble,
     you keep me safe;
     you stretch forth your hand
     your right hand shall save me.
8   You will make good your purpose to me.
     O God, your love endures for ever;
     do not abandon the works of your hands.

**antiphon**

*In the first verse, the psalmist exclaims that he or she will worship YHWH "before the gods," which caught my notice. The other psalms that mention divine beings only do so to proclaim that YHWH is superior to all other gods, not to suggest that other gods would be an audience to the psalmist's hymn. Since the second stanza mentions the kings of the earth, however, I wonder if there's a connection. Kings were certainly hailed as gods in ancient Egypt (and other places including, later, in Rome). Perhaps the psalmist is saying that YHWH's sovereignty take precedence over the sovereignty of the rulers of the earth, and that one day the earthly rulers will acknowledge this.*

## 139  To the leader. Of David. A Psalm.

1   God, you have searched me out and known me;
2   You know my sitting down and my rising up;
        you discern my thoughts from afar.
3   You trace my journeying and my resting
        and are acquainted with all my ways.
4   Indeed, there is not a word on my lips,
        but you, O God, know it altogether.
5   You press upon me behind and before
        and lay your hand upon me.
6   Such knowledge is too wonderful for me;
        it is a mystery I cannot fathom.

**antiphon**

7   Where can I go then from your Spirit?
    Where can I flee from your presence?
8   If I climb up to heaven, you are there;
        if I make the grave my bed, you are there.
9   If I take the wings of the morning
        and dwell in the uttermost parts of the sea,
10      even there your hand will lead me
        and your right hand hold me fast.
11  If I say, "Surely the darkness will cover me,
        and the light around me turn to night,"

12      darkness is not dark to you;
        night is as bright as day;
        darkness and light are the same.

**antiphon**

13  For you created my inmost parts;
        you knit me together in my mother's womb.
14  I thank you
        because I am wonderfully and fearfully made;
        your works are wonderful.
        I know it well.
15  My body was not hidden from you,
        while I was made in secret
        and woven in the depths of the earth.
16  Your eyes beheld my limbs, unfinished in the womb;
        they were written in your book;
        they were fashioned day by day,
        when as yet there was none of them.
17  How deep I find your thoughts, O God!
        how great is the sum of them!
18  I count them, but they number like sand;
        my life span would need to be like yours to count them.

**antiphon**

19  Oh, that you would slay the wicked, O God!
        You murderers, depart from me.
20      They speak despitefully against you;
        your enemies take your Name in vain.
21  Do I not hate those, O God, who hate you?
        and do I not loathe those who rise up against you?
22  I hate them with a perfect hatred;
        they have become my own enemies.
23  Search me out, O God, and know my heart;
        try me and know my restless thoughts.
24  See whether there is any wickedness in me
        and lead me in the way that is everlasting.

**antiphon**

*Verse 14 is one of my favorite verses in the book of Psalms. I love the idea that our creation is both wonderful and fear-inspiring, and that these two things are not opposites. I wrote this antiphon for a service at the end of new student orientation, my first year of seminary. For many of us, especially those who had left jobs and moved their families to answer their call, beginning seminary was both wonderful and frightening. I imagine this text will resonate with anyone who's gotten married, had children, taken monastic vows, or experienced other moments of profound transition.*

## 140  To the leader. A Psalm of David.

I know the Lord brings jus-tice for the poor.

1    Deliver me, O God, from evildoers;
         protect me from the violent,
2         who devise evil in their hearts
         and stir up strife all day long.
3    They have sharpened their tongues like serpents;
         adders' poison is on their lips.

**antiphon**

4    Keep me, O God, from the hands of the wicked;
         protect me from the violent,
         who are determined to make me fall.
5    The proud have hidden a snare for me
         and stretched out a net of cords;
         they have set traps for me along the path.
6    I have said to you, "You are my God;
         listen, O God, to my pleas for mercy.
7    O Most High God, the strength of my salvation,
         you cover my head in the day of battle.
8    Do not grant the desires of the wicked, O God,
         nor let their evil plans prosper.

**antiphon**

9    May those who surround me lift up their heads;
         let the evil of their lips overwhelm them.

10   May hot burning coals fall upon them;
          let them be cast into the mire, never to rise again."
11   May slanderers not be established on the earth,
          and evil shall hunt down the lawless.
12   I know that God will maintain the cause of the poor
          and render justice to the needy.
13   Surely, the righteous will give thanks to your Name,
          and the upright shall continue in your sight.

**antiphon**

   *As I've said in other places, I usually try to avoid "Lord" as a translation of YHWH,
but in this case it rhymed so nicely with "for" and "poor" that I felt it was worth using.*

## 141   A Psalm of David

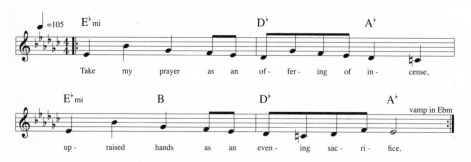

1    O God, I call to you; come to me quickly;
          hear my voice when I cry to you.
2    Let my prayer be set forth in your sight as incense,
          the lifting up of my hands as the evening sacrifice.
3    Set a watch before my mouth, O God,
          and guard the door of my lips;
4          let not my heart incline to any evil thing.
          let me not be occupied in wickedness
          with evildoers,
          nor eat of their choice foods.
5    Let the righteous strike me in friendly rebuke,
          and let the faithful correct me;
          let not the oil of the unrighteous anoint my head.
     My prayer is continually against their wicked deeds.

6   Let their judges be overthrown in stony places,
        that they may know my words are true.
7   As when a plowman turns over the earth in furrows,
        let their bones be scattered at the mouth of Sheol.

**antiphon**

8   But my eyes are turned to you, Most High God;
        in you I take refuge; do not strip me of my life.
9   Protect me from the snare they have laid for me
        and from the traps of the evildoers.
10  Let the wicked fall into their own nets,
        while I escape.

**antiphon**

*Given the way that Christians ignore all the laws about sacrifices and temple worship, it's good to know that at least one psalmist in the Bible thought that prayer was a sufficient alternative to animal sacrifice.*

## 142   A Maskil of David. When he was in the cave. A Prayer.

You are my re - fuge, all I have in the land of the liv - ing.

1   I cry to God with my voice;
        to God I make loud supplication.
2   I pour out my complaint
        and tell all my trouble.
3       when my spirit languishes within me.
    You know my path;
        they have hidden a trap for me where I walk.
4   Look at my right hand
        I have no friend;
        I have no refuge;
        no one cares for me.

**antiphon**

5    I cry out to you, O God;
        I say, "You are my refuge,
        all I have in the land of the living."
6    Listen to my cry for help, for I have been brought very low;
        save me from those who pursue me,
        for they are too strong for me.
7    Free me from prison,
        that I may give thanks to your Name.
     When you have dealt bountifully with me,
        the righteous will gather around me.

**antiphon**

*I'm not sure which cave the superscription is talking about. In 1 Samuel 22–24, David hides in a variety of caves and strongholds while being pursued by Saul. Eventually, Saul stops in a cave to relieve himself without realizing that David is hiding in the back. David sneaks up behind him and cuts off a corner of his robe to show that, although he could have killed Saul, he chose not to, proving his loyalty and saving Saul from a rather undignified death. And somehow, in the midst of it all, he found time to write a poem about the experience.*

## 143   A Psalm of David.

Do not judge your ser - vant, for no one is right - eous be - fore you.

1    God, hear my prayer,
        in your faithfulness heed my plea;
        answer me in your righteousness.
2    Enter not into judgment with your servant,
        for in your sight no creature is justified.
3    My enemy has hounded me
        and has crushed me to the ground,
        making me dwell in darkness
        like those who are long dead.
4    My spirit faints within me;
        my heart within me is desolate.

5    I remember the time past;
        I muse upon all your deeds;
        I consider the works of your hands.

6    I spread out my hands to you;
        I gasp for you like thirsty land.

**antiphon**

7    O God, answer me quickly;
        my spirit fails.
    Do not hide your face from me
        or I shall be like those who go down to the Pit.

8    Let me hear of your loving-kindness in the morning,
        for I put my trust in you;
        show me the road I must walk,
        for in you I set my hope.

9    Deliver me from my enemies, O God,
        for I flee to you for refuge.

10  Teach me to do what pleases you,
        for you are my God;
    Let your good Spirit lead me
        on level ground.

11  Revive me, O God, for your Name's sake;
        for your righteousness' sake, bring me out of trouble.

12  Of your goodness, destroy my enemies
        and bring all my foes to naught,
        for truly I am your servant.

**antiphon**

*This is the last of the Penitential Psalms, and begging God to not judge too harshly (v. 2) and asking for guidance for the future (v. 10) seems an appropriate way to end a confession. If you have an adventurous group of singers, I highly recommend checking out the choral settings of the seven Penitential Psalms by Renaissance composer Orlande de Lassus (*Psalmi Davidis Poenitentiales*). Even if you don't have a choir, you should find a recording and give them a listen—it makes great ambience for a service of meditative prayer.*

## 144 Of David.

Hap - py are those on whom such bles - sings fall.

Hap - py are those whose God is Yah - weh. *vamp in Eb*

1  Blessed be God, my rock!
    who trains my hands to fight
    and my fingers to battle;
2  My help and my fortress,
    my haven and my deliverer,
    my shield in whom I trust,
    who subdues the peoples under me.


**antiphon**


3  O God, what are we that you should care for us?
    mere mortals that you should think of us?
4  We are like a puff of wind;
    our days are like a passing shadow.
5  Bow your heavens, O God, and come down;
    touch the mountains, and they shall smoke.
6  Hurl the lightning and scatter them;
    shoot out your arrows and rout them.
7  Stretch out your hand from on high;
    rescue me and deliver me from the great waters,
    from the hand of foreign peoples
8     whose mouths speak lies
    and whose right hand is raised in falsehood.


**antiphon**


9  O God, I will sing to you a new song;
    I will play to you on a ten-stringed lyre.
10    You give victory to rulers
    and have rescued David, your servant,

11      from the deadly sword
     Deliver me from the hand of foreign peoples,
        whose mouths speak lies
        and whose right hand is raised in falsehood.

**antiphon**

12   May our sons be like plants
        nurtured from their youth,
        and our daughters like sculptured cornerstones
        cut for a palace.
13   May our barns be filled to overflowing
        with all manner of crops;
        may the flocks in our pastures
        increase by thousands and tens of thousands;
14      may our cattle be fat and sleek.
     May there be no breaching of the walls, no going into exile,
        no wailing in the streets.

**antiphon**

15   Happy are the people of whom this is so!
        happy are the people whose God is YHWH!

**antiphon**

     *The trouble with translating both* אֱלֹהִים *(elohim) and* יְהוָה *(YHWH) as "God" is that sometimes you run into verses like verse 15. Rendering* שֶׁיְהוָה אֱלֹהָיו *as "whose God is God" is clunky and misses the original intent. Since the psalmists felt no qualms about using the name of God in their poems and songs, I've decided to do so here, even if it means that this antiphon will never be used by my Jewish friends.*

## 145 Praise. Of David.

1    I will exalt you, my God and king,
        and bless your Name forever.

2    Every day will I bless you
        and praise your Name forever.

3    Great is God and greatly to be praised;
        there is no end to your greatness.

4    One generation shall praise your works to another
        and shall declare your power.

5    I will ponder the glorious splendor of your majesty
        and all your marvelous works.

6    They shall speak of the might of your wondrous acts,
        and I will tell of your greatness.

7    They shall publish the remembrance of your great goodness;
        they shall sing of your righteous deeds.

**antiphon**

8    God is gracious and full of compassion,
        slow to anger and of great kindness.

9    God is loving to everyone
        and compassion is over all God's works.

10    All your works praise you, O God,
        and your faithful servants bless you.

**antiphon**

11    They make known the glory of your kingship
        and speak of your power;

12         that the peoples may know of your power
        and the glorious splendor of your kingship.

13 Your kingship is everlasting;
   your dominion endures throughout all ages.

**antiphon**

   God is faithful in all words
      and merciful in all deeds.
14 God upholds all those who fall;
      and lifts up those bowed down.
15 The eyes of all wait upon you, O God,
      and you give them their food in due season.
16 You open wide your hand
      and satisfy the needs of every living creature.

**antiphon**

17 God is righteous in all ways
      and loving in all works.
18 God is near to those who call,
      to all who call faithfully.
19 God fulfills the desire of those who fear;
      God hears their cries and helps them.
20 God preserves all those who love,
      but destroys all the wicked.
21 My mouth shall speak the praise of God;
      let all flesh bless the holy Name forever and ever.

**antiphon**

*This final psalm of David is quite cleverly constructed. The overarching theme of this psalm is the "kingship of God," a theme that is especially pronounced in verses 11–13. This is also an acrostic psalm, and the first letter of each verse spells out the Hebrew alphabet, with the mysterious omission of the letter "נ," which should go between verses 13 and 14. (The English version in most Bibles includes the missing two lines—verse 13b—that are not in the Hebrew but are found in the Septuagint.)*

*Interestingly, verses 11, 12, and 13 start with the letters מ, ל, כ, (m, l, k, just like in English). When written backwards, this spells מֶלֶךְ, the Hebrew word for king. Since one letter is omitted, this places verses 10–11 at the exact center of the psalm, making the "kingship of God" central to the psalm in more ways than one.*

**146**

Hal - le - lu - jah! Do not put your trust in prin - ces.

Hal - le - lu - jah! Our hope is in our God.

1    Hallelujah!
         Praise God, O my soul!
2    I will praise God as long as I live;
         I will sing praises to my God while I have my being.


**antiphon**


3    Put not your trust in rulers, nor in any child of earth,
         for there is no help in them.
4    When they breathe their last,
             they return to earth,
             and in that day their thoughts perish.


**antiphon**


5    Happy are they who have the God of Jacob for their help!
         whose hope is in God, their God;
6    Who made heaven and earth,
             the seas, and all that is in them,
             who keeps promises forever,
7        who gives justice to those who are oppressed,
             and food to those who hunger.
     God sets the prisoners free;
8        God opens the eyes of the blind
             and lifts up those bowed down;
             God loves the righteous.
9        God cares for the stranger
             and sustains the orphan and widow,
             but frustrates the way of the wicked.


**antiphon**

10   God shall reign forever,
       your God, O Zion, throughout all generations.
       Hallelujah!

**antiphon**

*With this psalm, we've reached the beginning of the end of the Psalter. The last five psalms of the Psalter are jubilant and triumphant; each begins and ends with the word "Hallelujah" (הַלְלוּ־יָהּ), which is Hebrew for "Praise God." As a unit, they are recited each morning as part of Shacharit, the Jewish daily morning prayer service, and I've tried to write the music so that the five psalms, when taken together, form a satisfying arc.*

*This psalm in particular is one of my favorites, with its promises of hope for the downtrodden, food for the hungry, and justice for the oppressed. It sounds quite a bit like Jesus' summary of Isaiah in Luke 4.*

## 147

Je - ho - vah with im - meas - ur - able wis - dom calls each star by name.

1   Hallelujah!
    How good it is to sing praises to our God!
       how pleasant to sing glorious praise!

**antiphon**

2   God rebuilds Jerusalem;
       and gathers the exiles of Israel.
3   God heals the brokenhearted
       and binds up their wounds.
4   God counts the number of the stars
       and calls them all by names.
5   Great is our God and mighty in power;
       there is no limit to God's wisdom.
6   God lifts up the lowly,
       but casts the wicked to the ground.

**antiphon**

7   Sing to God with thanksgiving;
        make music on the harp to our God,
8       who covers the heavens with clouds
        and prepares rain for the earth,
        who makes grass grow upon the mountains
        and green plants to serve humanity,
9       who provides food for flocks and herds
        and for the young ravens when they cry.
10  God is not impressed by the might of horses
        and does not value the strength of people,
11      God has pleasure in those who fear him,
        in those who await gracious favor.

**antiphon**

12  Worship God, O Jerusalem;
        praise your God, O Zion;
13  For God has strengthened the bars of your gates;
        and has blessed your children within you.
14  God has established peace on your borders;
        and satisfies you with the finest wheat.

**antiphon**

15  God sends out a command to the earth,
        and word runs very swiftly.
16  God gives snow like wool;
        and scatters hoarfrost like ashes.
17  God scatters hail like bread crumbs;
        who can stand against the cold?
18  God sends forth a word and melts them;
        God blows wind, and waters flow.
19  God declares to Jacob
        statutes and judgments for Israel.
20  God has not done so to any other nation;
        to them God has not revealed judgments.
        Hallelujah!

**antiphon**

This is one of the first antiphons I wrote. I'd just graduated with my undergrad music degree and had been invited to lead music for the Columbia University Episcopal Chaplaincy. I was just beginning to play around with Hebrew and decided that for this antiphon, I would translate YHWH as "Jehovah" rather than "Lord." If you're interested, the Jewish tradition puts the vowels from "adonay" into YHWH (to remind the reader that they shouldn't say the word out loud), resulting in "yahowah." In German, Js are pronounced like English Ys, and Ws are pronounced like English Vs, so the nineteenth-century German Protestants who pioneered this area of scholarship transliterated God's name from "yahowah" into "Jahovah."

I considered rewriting this antiphon with a different word but ultimately decided to leave it in for variety. Despite its historical inaccuracy, "Jehovah" is still a prettier word than "God."

## 148

Praise the name of the Lord, whose splen-dor is o-ver earth and hea-ven!

1   Hallelujah!
    Praise God from the heavens;
        praise God in the heights.
2   Praise God, all you angels;
        praise God, all the host.
3   Praise God, sun and moon;
        praise God, you shining stars.
4   Praise God, heaven of heavens,
        and you waters above the heavens.
5   Let them praise the Name of God;
        who commanded that they be created.
6   God made them stand fast forever and ever;
        and gave them a law which shall not pass away.

**antiphon**

7   Praise God from the earth,
        you sea-monsters and all deeps,
8       fire and hail, snow and fog,
        tempestuous wind, doing God's will,

9      mountains and hills,
         fruit trees and cedars;
10     wild beasts and cattle,
         creeping things and winged birds,
11     rulers of the Earth and all peoples,
         judges and rulers of the world;
12     young men and maidens,
         old and young together.
13  Let them praise the Name of God,
      whose Name only is exalted,
      whose splendor is over earth and heaven.
14  God has raised up strength for his people
      and praise for loyal servants,
      the children of Israel, a people who are near him.
      Hallelujah!

**antiphon**

*I first wrote this melody in 7/8 but quickly found that putting it into 4/4 made it much more singable. If you want to hear what it first sounded like, just remove the fifth eighth note of every bar. I do not recommend using a tune in 7/8 for processionals, though—people will be tripping all over themselves.*

## 149

Let the faith-ful re-joice in tri-umph. Let them be joy-ful on their beds.

1    Hallelujah!
    Sing to God a new song;
       sing praise in the congregation of the faithful.
2    Let Israel rejoice in its Maker;
       let the children of Zion be joyful in their sovereign.
3    Let them praise the Name in the dance;
       let them sing praise with timbrel and harp.
4    For God takes pleasure in people
       and adorns the poor with victory.

**antiphon**

5   Let the faithful rejoice in triumph;
        let them be joyful on their beds.
6       Let the praises of God be in their throat
        and a two-edged sword in their hand
7       to wreak vengeance on the nations
        and punishment on the peoples,
8       binding their rulers in chains
        and their nobles with links of iron,
9       inflicting on them the judgment decreed.
    This is glory for all the faithful.
        Hallelujah!

**antiphon**

*Verse 5 struck my fancy. Does it imply that people routinely slept in the Temple? Is it referring to ritual prostration? Does it mean that God should be praised at home as well as in the Temple? Or does it just find something inherently joyful about being in bed?*

## 150

Ha - le - lu - jah, Ha - le - lu - jah!   Ha - le - lu - jah, Ha - le - lu - jah!

1   Hallelujah!
    Praise God in the holy temple;
        praise God in the firmament of power.
2   Praise God for mighty acts;
        praise God for excellent greatness.
3   Praise God with the blast of the ram's-horn;
        praise God with lyre and harp.
4   Praise God with timbrel and dance;
        praise God with strings and pipe.
5   Praise God with resounding cymbals;
        praise God with loud-clanging cymbals.
6   Let everything that has breath praise the Lord.
        Hallelujah!

**antiphon**

*The Psalter ends quite differently than it begins. While Psalm 1 conjured the image of a pious student sitting and studying the psalms, the last psalm conjures the image of a large gathering of people singing loudly and joyfully. Just as many individual psalms move from the individual to the communal, so does the Psalter as a whole. This psalm isn't a conclusion as much as it is an invitation to keep going; as Klaus Seybold says, the Psalter ends with a colon rather than a period. So keep going! Keep singing! And try writing some of your own psalms along the way. . . .*

# Bibliography

Berry, Mary. "Psalmody." *A New Dictionary of Liturgy & Worship*. Edited by J. G. Davies. London: SCM Press, 1986.

Carroll, J. W. *Mainline to the Future: Congregations for the 21st Century*. Louisville, KY: Westminster John Knox Press, 2000.

Crossan, John Dominic. *Who Killed Jesus?: Exposing the Roots of Anti-Semitism in the Gospel Story of the Death of Jesus*. San Francisco: HarperSanFranciso, 1996.

Driver, Tom F. *Liberating Rites: Understanding the Transformative Power of Ritual*. Boulder, CO: Westview Press, 1998.

Ferrara, Lawrence. *Philosophy and the Analysis of Music: Bridges to Musical Sound, Form, and Reference*. New York: Excelsior Music Publishing Co., 1991.

Finke, Roger. "Innovative Returns to Tradition: Using Core Teachings as the Foundation for Innovative Accommodation." *Journal for the Scientific Study of Religion*, 41, no. 1 (March 2004). p19-34.

Gibbs, Eddie, and Ryan K. Bolger. *Emerging Churches: Creating Christian Community in Postmodern Cultures*. Grand Rapids, MI: Baker Academic, 2005.

Gillingham, S. E. *The Poems and Psalms of the Hebrew Bible*. Oxford: Oxford University Press, 1994.

Harper, John. "Psalmody." *The New Westminster Dictionary of Liturgy and Worship*. Edited by Paul Bradshaw. Louisville, KY: Westminster John Knox Press, 2002.

Hirsch, Emil G. "Psalms." *Jewish Encyclopedia*. 1906. Ed. Cyrus Adler, et al., February 11, 2008. http://www.jewishencyclopedia.com.

Holladay, William L. *The Psalms through Three Thousand Years: Prayerbook of a Cloud of Witnesses*. Minneapolis, MN: Fortress, 1993.

Jones, Tony. *The New Christians: Dispatches from the Emergent Frontier*. San Francisco: Jossey-Bass, 2008.

Limburg, James. "Psalms, Book of." *The Anchor Bible Dictionary: Volume 5*. New York: Doubleday, 1992.

McCann, J. Clinton, Jr. "The Book of Psalms: Introduction, Commentary, and Reflections." *The New Interpreter's Bible: Volume 4*. Nashville: Abingdon Press, 1996.

McKnight, Scot. "Five Streams of the Emerging Church; Key Elements of the Most Controversial and Misunderstood Movement in the Church Today." *Christianity Today* 51, no. 2 (Fall 2007): 34–39.

Mitchell, Nathan D. "Reforms, Protestant and Catholic." *The Oxford History of Christian Worship*. Edited by Geoffrey Wainwright and Karen B. Westerfield Tucker. Oxford: Oxford University Press, 2006.

Mowinckel, Sigmund. *The Psalms in Israel's Worship*. Sheffield, England: JSOT Press, 1992.

Nowell, I. "Psalms, Book of." *New Catholic Encyclopedia: Volume 11*. 2nd ed. Edited by Berard L. Marthaler. Detroit: Gale Group, 2003.

Otten, Joseph. "Antiphon." *The Catholic Encyclopedia, Volume I*. New York: Robert Appleton Company, 1907.

Schuman, Niek A. "Paschal Liturgy and Psalmody in Jerusalem 380–384 CE: Some Observations and Implications." *Psalms and Liturgy*. Edited by Dirk J. Human and Cas J. A. Vos. London: T&T Clark International, 2004.

Seybold, Klaus. *Introducing the Psalms*. London: T&T Clark, 1990.

Shepherd, Massey H., Jr. *The Psalms in Christian Worship: A Practical Guide*. Minneapolis, MN: Augsburg Publishing House, 1976.

Thibodeau, Timothy. "Western Christendom." *The Oxford History of Christian Worship*. Edited by Geoffrey Wainwright and Karen B. Westerfield Tucker. Oxford: Oxford University Press, 2006.

Tolson, Jay. "A Return to Tradition: A New Interest in Old Ways Takes Root in Catholicism and Many Other Faiths." *U.S. News & World Report*, December 13, 2007.

White, Susan J. *Foundations of Christian Worship*. Louisville, KY: Westminster John Knox Press, 2006.

Winner, Lauren F. "Gen X Revisited: A Return to Tradition?" *Christian Century* 117, no. 31 (November 8, 2000): 1146–48.